POCKET
MONEY TO
PROPERTY

HANNAH McQUEEN
POCKET MONEY TO PROPERTY

HOW TO CREATE
FINANCIALLY INDEPENDENT KIDS

ALLEN&UNWIN
SYDNEY • MELBOURNE • AUCKLAND • LONDON

To Mum and Dad—thank you.
To Cameron and Madison—listen up.

First published in 2017

Allen & Unwin
Level 3, 228 Queen Street
Auckland 1010, New Zealand
Phone: (64 9) 377 3800

Email: info@allenandunwin.com
Web: www.allenandunwin.co.nz

83 Alexander Street
Crows Nest NSW 2065, Australia
Phone: (61 2) 8425 0100

A catalogue record for this book is available
from the National Library of New Zealand

ISBN 978 1 877505 83 6

Internal design and figures by Kate Barraclough
Set in 10.5pt/15pt Sabon
Printed and bound in Australia by Griffin Press

10 9 8 7 6 5 4 3 2 1

CONTENTS

CONTENTS

INTRODUCTION

We are facing one of the most uncertain economic times in the history of the developed world. The motto is 'too big to fail', the answer for mass overspending to print money. Consumerism, as a by-product of advertising, has infiltrated our subconscious. We are taught a sense of entitlement from such an early age. Schools are trying (unsuccessfully) to improve financial education, but unless teaching the consequences of financial choices is adhered to at home, all that our children are being taught is that it doesn't really matter. When the times are good you don't care, because rising property prices cover a multitude of financial sins. When times are bad . . . well, you just use your credit card.

Too many of us are taught that the world owes us a living and that the universe is on our side. Schools create an environment where we are taught that failure is bad and we can all be winners. I get it—it's admirable, to a degree—but it does little to prepare our kids for the brutality of the real world.

In the financial sense, it heavily disadvantages them. Don Draper, the iconic *Mad Men* character, was probably more realistic when he said the universe is indifferent. My experience with money has shown me that the world owes us nothing. It will be OK in the end if it's OK in the end.

However, for many of us, this won't be the case. I have worked with thousands of clients to help them get control of their money, kill their mortgages and sort their retirements, and for many of them the number-one drain on resources or distraction from future planning is an adult child who should be independent but is not. As a parent, the one non-negotiable cost that overrides any retirement goals is often to help your kids.

As we know, there are limited funds available for the government to pay pensions. Over the next generation, our parents will be forced to use all their equity to fund their own retirement. The government will run out of money, or significantly drop or delay the already meagre state pension. There will be no inheritance, no head-start or hand up. Our kids will be on their own. They will need to navigate their way through a quagmire of obstacles, but we can help them. We *need* to help them. We need to teach them because no one else will, and as we teach them we will probably learn a few things ourselves.

There are reasons why becoming financially independent is harder for kids today than it was in the past, and these reasons are discussed in subsequent chapters. Work is a four-letter word that fewer of our teenagers are experiencing before or during university, and that is putting them at a disadvantage for future employment. Student-loan sizes are epic and, for some, the process of going to university has only helped them realise that they no longer want a career in the path they had chosen. This is not bad or new, but the difference for our kids is that they have the privilege of a $60,000 loan in exchange for changing tack. But, if it is any consolation, today's kids seem to be better and brighter than us, and are evolving to be more agile and able to cope with change at a faster rate than we can. Some call them digital natives. But they are not financially smart or savvy.

Despite their ignorance, many are bold. They respect their elders if they are worthy of respect, not because they are told to respect them. They tend to scoff at hierarchy and think they are the first person to be philosophical or to understand psychology or social sciences in general. Their brashness is often interpreted as arrogance, but I am not sure that's the whole story. The media gives them a bad rap, and uses a broad brush to dismiss them.

But they will not be dismissed, and within the group of crazies there is a growing number who do want to do well in life and get ahead. They don't buy into the narcissism of the standard millennial stereotype. They are more grounded and are prepared to work hard. For these people, I write this book; for people like Anna and Asher, two students from my old high school to whom I have offered internships. There is no doubt in my mind that they are smarter than me. Inexperienced, but smarter. They will be better than me, and they deserve to be. My job as their mentor is to help them become what they are capable of being. I imagine it is a relief to their parents to have someone watching out for them, and I hope that someone will think to do it for my kids.

One of the lessons we learn is that before you know what you can be, sometimes you need to realise what you are not and should not be. Sometimes you must fail. Failure leads to innovation, growth and becoming more agile. (Well, it's supposed to.) But at the very least it creates necessity, and necessity creates invention.

Agility and adaptability are the most important concepts in the current landscape. They underpin successful entrepreneurship and radicalise the speed of change. Albert Einstein said 'a person who never made a mistake never tried anything new'. The problem, however, is our school system teaches our kids only how to succeed, and measures success with exams. This does not translate to the real world, on any meaningful level. The system is not designed to help our kids cope with life.

Certainly teenagers can be selfish—that's part of their rite of passage. Selfish, yes; misunderstood, probably; but stupid, no. (Well, some are. Usually the loudest ones.) They are just not sure how to succeed, because they also recognise that the school and university system barely equips them for adulthood. But they have been taught to think critically—which means if you are going to teach them you need to be sure that you can back up your claims with fact, research or proven examples; otherwise, they won't buy into it. This is possibly where most parents tap out because it feels hard, and it *is* hard.

Some of the topics I plan to cover in the coming chapters are genetics, biases and family influences on our financial behaviour, and how these tendencies need to be identified early so that they can be cultivated, or further skills developed to offset weaknesses or take advantage of opportunities.

I spend time discussing how you can identify and fan the flame of entrepreneurship; how financial hypocrisy won't cut it, especially if you are trying to impart financial truths; and what age-appropriate skills need to be taught and what your kids need to know to navigate through each financial stage.

Our girls in particular need to be taught about money differently. Because of their upbringing, the women I work with tend to be more romantic than practical about money. Many of them don't feel confident talking about it, and are scared of rocking the boat. Most are in an average relationship or feel financially exposed because they don't want to discuss money with their spouse, or they have married a financial dud. We need to give our girls the knowledge and confidence to manage their own finances, and to be successful givers, rather than just trying to please everybody.

Our financial landscape is moving fast, and our kids are getting left behind. This book will help you equip your child for the real world, which means the financial world. Money, after all, underpins it all.

PART I
TOWARDS FINANCIALLY INDEPENDENT KIDS

CHAPTER 1
THE UNIQUE CHALLENGES FACING OUR YOUTH

WHY IT'S SO HARD FOR KIDS TODAY

Today, there are financial challenges facing our kids that will affect them for years to come. New Zealand society has:

- the highest number of people under 30 becoming bankrupt
- kids living at home for longer than is healthy
- parents being slow to sort their own retirement
- parents unsure about what is helping their kids, and what is enabling their 'averageness'
- kids starting their adult lives in debt
- a generation of kids who don't believe they can get ahead, so they don't bother trying.

As parents, we can see that our kids are more likely to experience downward mobility, which means they are likely to be less well off than we are. Back in the day, to become financially independent you just needed to work hard, go to university, get a job, buy a house, pay off the mortgage and save for your retirement. If you ticked all the boxes along the way, you could be fairly certain that you would work through the stages and be fine by the end.

This is not the case now. Going to university does not mean you'll get a job. Having a job doesn't mean you will progress. Having a high-paying job does not mean you will actually get ahead. Most young people today won't be buying their first property until they are in their late thirties, if ever—that is, if they have even bothered to move out of home by then.

A lot of our kids will incur a student loan for the privilege of discovering that they didn't even want to work in that particular field. The size of the loan will be a financial burden that seems impossible to pay off, or simply not worth their while to try. With this backdrop, many parents feel the need to mother their adult children, not transitioning them to becoming financially independent adults.

We also know that, as they transition to adulthood, our kids will live in uncertain financial times. Not just because jobs are changing, or because of technological advances—these are part of the new normal. The times are uncertain because the financial tide is going out, which means those swimming naked can no longer hide. But as any surfer worth their salt knows, some beaches produce their best waves on an outgoing tide.

Social media tends to create a lot of envy. Most kids don't grasp that people only post the very best versions of themselves. Kids are seeing who has what, or who's doing what with whom. As parents, we are not sure how to combat this, as media and society in general tend to disempower us and our role.

We know we want our kids to be financially independent. As parents, we want them to be better and do better than us, and to live a satisfying and full life. Money underpins this. Yet we don't speak about money honestly.

We understand that our role as the parent is to provide the foundation for our children to lead a full and happy life, but we seldom dig deeper to addresses the financial foundation, despite it being a key input for the output of authentic happiness.

Some parents don't talk about money because they believe it will subvert their kids' values, and make them too interested in it. Nan J Morrison, who runs the Council for Economic Education in the United States, considers this view ignorant, and that this is turning an essential part of our daily lives into a 'dirty' topic. In my experience, not only is the fear of creating gold-digging kids misplaced, but older kids find it demeaning that such a vital part of life that they are eager to learn more about is brushed under the carpet.

As a parent, you want your kid to go to university, especially if that is their particular goal. The reality is, though, that means a 17-year-old has to make a decision about whether they should incur $50,000 to $100,000 of debt in the process. The person making the decision is a teenager, who is inexperienced at life and whose brain is still underdeveloped. The prefrontal cortex doesn't have the same functional capacity at 17 as it does at 25. This means many teenagers make impulsive decisions without being able to fully grasp the effects of different choices.

They have no idea what the jobs are like in the field they are studying for. They tend to be told they need two degrees, not one, as one degree no longer ensures them a job at the other end (I can tell you that two degrees doesn't either). They are told that technology is changing so quickly that the jobs they might work in once qualified haven't been invented yet or might no longer exist. Both comments are at least partly true, but are more a form of scaremongering than actual help.

Kids are making decisions on careers without knowing what they might like to do for a job, or what they might earn. Their career choice has little connection to the money that is needed to fund the lifestyle they are wanting to live. This was OK in the days when you would come out of university with a student loan of $20,000. But $50,000 to $100,000—well, that is not OK. They don't understand the financial reality of adult life and they make their decisions in ignorance.

I do feel sorry for us as parents. But as a financial advisor, something has to give. Children need to be taught to be purposeful and conditioned for what the real world is like, and parents need to play a positive role in this. At the very least, a parent needs to put their hand up to say 'I haven't tried to' or 'I can't' fulfil this role, and outsource the lesson-giving to someone who can. But do not leave your kids exposed to these problems without taking some steps to help them.

You do not need to be financially successful to teach your kids about money. But you do need to be honest. You need to understand what you have done wrong and how you have learned to do things better, or what you are planning on doing to sort things out.

In my opinion, kids need to know how to save by the age of 10, an art form that is practised through their teenage years. They need to master an allowance and have an idea of where they are going by 14. Financial terms and options need to be presented so that they are not taken out by consumerism and credit once they leave school. They need to understand what their life is going to cost, what their career is likely to pay and how they will bridge the gap. More and more people will become self-employed over the next 10 years, which means your kids need an understanding of business.

Back in the day, you could rely on life correcting extreme views. University was the first great equaliser, as your parents' wealth or connections didn't benefit you. If you had been unpopular at school, you were no longer alone, as there were plenty of other odd bods who were happy enough to join forces.

The next great equaliser was getting a job, working for someone, then having a family. By that point most of your ignorant and sharp edges were well and truly smoothed over by life. If you had taken a few wrong turns early on, it was seldom a barrier to later being able to catch up.

You could take some comfort that life's lessons would straighten you out, and then you would be on track. Once you were on the right track, then you would take comfort that that track would eventually take you to your destination of being able to live a life you enjoy.

Now, fewer people are getting on track early enough to increase the odds in their favour, and being on track is no longer a given that you will end up where you want to be. Our kids are facing financial uncertainty, and the way to combat that is through financial insight and coaching. We must equip our kids for adulthood, which at the very least will mean they are not living with us for the rest of their lives. But beyond that, we want them to be financially successful.

WHAT IS FINANCIAL SUCCESS?

If financial success is the destination, we need to understand what that actually means, so we can be sure we have achieved it.

FINANCIAL SUCCESS (NOUN)

Living a life you enjoy. In control of your money, with a plan to ensure your retirement is sorted. To be at peace with your finances. To have a shared financial goal with your partner. To have created financially independent children. Not measured as an amount, but as a destination. To be financially successful is to be socially responsible.

Synonyms: Happy, in control, purposeful

Antonyms: Anxious, socially irresponsible, aimless

Financial success is the sum of a number of things that, as a parent, you must teach your children:

- How money underpins almost everything, including relationships.
- The bank is not, and will never be, their friend. It can be a business partner, but the bank will take its cut.
- Buy a house as soon as they can.
- Pay off the mortgage as fast as they can.
- What financial success means.
- How to spend less than they earn.
- How to set up and operate a bank account.
- How to ask for the discount.
- What is their money personality and what risks it exposes them to.
- That their ability to earn money will always be their best asset, and that the ability to make money on money is their best ally.

- If you are running behind, or want to jump ahead, leverage is your friend.

Then there are some other, less obviously financially related, things:

- Encourage your kids to understand what makes them happy.
- Teach them the rules of the game. Show them how to play it better than everyone else.
- Cultivate their strengths.
- Develop their entrepreneurial tendencies.
- Teach your son to respect women and be willing to share the household load.
- Teach your daughter to take charge of her life and not always try to please other people.

Most importantly, lead by example. How do you expect your kids to engage, if you don't?

Talking honestly and openly with our kids about money is harder than it might seem. It's challenging no matter what socio-economic level you're on. Affluent parents, who have more money than they need, will be trying to set limits for their kids—their decisions around what to spend money on, how much and when to stop are more emotional than financial. Middle- and working-class parents are usually living pay-day to pay-day, while trying to provide the greatest opportunities and most enriching life to their kids. But there can also be an emotional side to this. Kids can see that their parents might not earn as much as other families, and the conclusions they can draw from this observation can be damaging, both to their relationship with their parents and how they see themselves in the world.

MY CHILDHOOD

I had a good childhood. We grew up in an average home. I don't remember wanting for anything but I also don't remember there being spare money. My parents worked hard. Mum probably worked the hardest and most consistently. Dad was self-employed, which meant sometimes his income was good and then it wasn't.

It's funny the things you remember about your childhood. My mum used to say that I am an educated version of my father. I took that as a compliment, although on reflection I am not entirely sure it was meant as one!

I would describe my mum as a conscientious saver with a penchant for cushions. My dad could survive on the smell of an oily rag. He still can—all he needs are Weet-Bix, surfboard wax and the occasional trip to the bakery. (In fact, if you want to put him in a good mood, just let him go surfing and pick up a Sally Lunn on the way home, and he'll be content.)

My parents were both savers. Mum went without to make sure that we had what we needed. She taught me how to budget, how to balance a cheque book, how to shop for a bargain. I saw in action what conscientious effort could do.

Oddly enough, though, I have a different money personality to my parents. I am a shopper. I didn't realise this tendency until I started to earn my own money. As quickly as I earned it, I felt entitled to spend it. The more time-poor I became, the more treats I felt I deserved.

By the time I reached my seventeenth birthday, I was in possession of a full driver's licence. I had finished sixth form (Year 12) and wasn't sure if I wanted to hang around for the seventh. I decided to leave home in Havelock North and head to Auckland, one month after turning 17. I remember my red Fiat

Uno was packed with all my possessions, including a second-hand microwave my Mum had picked up for me the week before, and my ghetto blaster. I was trying to be brave, my mum was trying to be staunch, Dad was crying. I hugged them goodbye. Dad said he was proud of me. Mum whispered something, possibly to herself more than to me. She said, 'I hope I have taught you enough to do well. I hope I have prepared you for adulthood.' I am not sure if I replied.

So I was lucky enough to have had a good childhood. Now I have my own children, I want them to have a good childhood too.

More importantly, I want them to have a great adulthood. Let's face it, there is no point in peaking too soon.

Money underpins everything. If you master money, you are halfway to a great adulthood. The question all parents need to ask is, have I prepared my children for a successful adulthood? Have I done enough so that they won't suffer 'failure to launch'?

CHILDHOOD AND THE ROLE OF THE PARENT

I have always assumed that where there are children, there must be a childhood, a time in their life where they are not bound by the rules of society, and can essentially 'run free'. Then I read a book by Neil Postman, *The Disappearance of Childhood*, in which he challenged this belief, claiming the idea of childhood is a relatively new concept that emerged in the seventeenth century.

In the eighteenth century the idea of childhood started to take the form with which we are familiar. Up until that time, children as young as six simply were not regarded as fundamentally different from adults. A child went from infancy to adulthood; there was no transition period that we now call 'childhood'. While it was recognised that children were physically smaller than adults, this fact did not give them any special status. Historian J.H. Plumb puts it: 'There was no separate world of childhood.' So while I loved my childhood, the whole idea of *having* a childhood is a relatively recent phenomenon, but one I will come back to later in this book.

The social construction of childhood also began less than 300 years ago. Between 1750 and 1814, 2400 children's books were published, when prior to that there had been almost none. The eighteenth century was when children's clothing was introduced, education was designed especially for children, and children's crimes were distinguished from adults' crimes. Children's games like dice and jigsaws were invented. It was just prior to this that John Locke, the great English philosopher, produced some enlightened thinking. His work *Some Thoughts Concerning Education,* which was first published in 1693, went through 25 editions in the eighteenth century. Most of all, Locke furthered the theory of childhood through his now well-known idea that at birth the mind is a blank tablet or slate. A heavy responsibility then falls on the parents as to what is written on their child's mind. It could be said that an ignorant, shameless, undisciplined child represented the failures of adults, not of the child. As I was researching this point, I could not help but reflect as to what I had allowed, and am allowing, to be written on my own children's minds (a scary thought!).

Sigmund Freud, in *The Interpretation of Dreams* (published in 1899), didn't wholly buy into a child's mind being a blank canvas at birth. Instead, he claimed that we all have instinctive psychological drives. To achieve mature adulthood, children must overcome, outgrow and sublimate their instinctual passions. Freud also reaffirmed Locke: he believed the earliest interactions between a child and parent were decisive in determining the kind of adult the child would become.

So as you can see, the onus is on us as parents to mould our children's relationship with money so they can achieve financial success for themselves. To help diagnose their money personalities. To better understand where their strengths and challenges will lie. To teach and train them in the art of money, to better the chances of their own financial success, and your own.

KRYPTONITE AND THE SUN

I remember watching the Superman movies when I was a kid. I loved them. Clark Kent was a great guy, who had an even greater alter-ego. He was handsome, brave and fell in love with a good woman. He got the girl and saved the day—everything I need in a movie!

When I watched the more recent version of *Superman* with my seven-year-old son, I looked at it differently. I saw it from a parent's perspective: aware that your child may have a talent that could work for him or against him; that your child has an obligation to do the right thing for themselves and the wider world; that while you can teach them everything you know, you are aware of what they are up against, how heavy the weight is that will rest on their shoulders. I loved the metaphor of good versus evil; the idea that if you want something there will usually be something or someone (in Clark's case, Lex Luthor) who will make it harder than it needs to be—but who makes you better than you thought you could be. You will always have weaknesses, but you have to know them before you can combat them.

Superman came from the planet Krypton. 'Krypton' derives from the Greek word for 'hidden'. Within the core of the planet was the element kryptonite. Kryptonite was originally depicted as a red substance, but was later changed to a bright green colour. According to Wikipedia, kryptonite is a fictional radioactive mineral that drains Superman of his strength while at the same time giving humans superhuman powers. Kryptonite is Superman's weakness. He needs to stay the hell away from it or, if exposed to it, wait for the sun to recharge his cells.

I don't know much more about Superman's story, and I apologise to DC Comics fans for my over-simplification. However, the point that I am trying to make is that Superman's Achilles' heel was found in his home—the very planet that he came from.

Financial success is underpinned by the same principles. You can't always help your financial weaknesses—they will be what they will be. But how you deal with them is learned. Skills are taught and developed.

Parents have the responsibility to set up their children for financial success, but usually they become their child's form of kryptonite, undermining the child's chance at financial success by their own actions, inactions or ineffective communication. You need to help them find their sun.

In doing my research for this book, I have concluded that common sense when it comes to money is not all that common. This is possibly because we teach our kids the areas in which we feel competent, which is great. But we ignore the areas where we don't. Too many adults are financially inept, so by default their kids are not being taught the tools for financial success.

We know that kids are sponges, soaking up everything around them, so as parents we need to be intentional in what surrounds them. Family therapist, counsellor and parenting coach Diane Levy articulates this beautifully when she says, 'Our job as a parent is to help our children to do things that they find difficult, but not impossible. So that they have the joy of mastery, and so that their self-esteem will increase.'

Your kids will learn from you the value of earning, how to manage money, whether you should care about your financial future, whether saving is a priority, whether you can change your financial outcome, if you even need to care about the financial impact of decisions, how money can create happiness, and whether delayed gratification even exists. The reality, however, is that they are more likely to learn this from what you *don't* do, as opposed to what you do. The weakness with this is that kids are most likely to draw the wrong conclusions. American businessman and speaker Dave Ramsey says much of the financial education a kid receives is 'caught' not taught. This means that what you do is so much more important than what you say.

TODAY'S PARENTS

Today's parents are no less capable or caring than their parents or grandparents, but the way we parent has changed. With change comes improvement—and some weaknesses. Our kids face a lot of the same challenges we did, but also a whole lot of different ones, unlike most generations before. They are exposed to some adult concepts younger than they should be, while other, more necessary, life skills seem to get missed out altogether.

Today's parents read more and are keen to equip themselves with 'tools'. But when I spoke to John Cowan of The Parenting Place, he agreed that the plethora of information available to parents, across a number of topics, can create confusion, which ultimately leads to paralysis. He believes that some parents are 'ironing a crease into their character of their kids', which can translate to poor financial behaviour. His feeling is that parents are generally trying to do well—parenting more intentionally—and for the most part are succeeding, but this doesn't tend to cross over to developing financially able kids. Many parents are confused about how to give their kids a good financial education.

Cowan observes that if parents are too anxious, they can't sow confidence and a 'let's get into life' attitude in their kids. Excessive anxiousness erodes the resilience of our kids. Children very quickly pick up on parents' anxieties and absorb them into their own fears and behaviours.

One of the most common areas of anxiousness in the home is around finances, or lack of financial progress. How this plays out is different for each family, but it can be said that when you are not in control of your money you are not in control of your life, and your children are aware of this on some level. The worst conclusion your child can make, though, is that this can't be changed. Past financial results do not suggest your future capability. The two are seldom linked. Your past behaviour and results reflect where you would land if you didn't try—which is not a particularly helpful measure when trying to determine how high you can fly.

Teaching your kids how to be financially successful tends to be a bit of an afterthought. While researching this book, I was disappointed at the lack of 'meat' around money and finance for kids. Most books seem to break down successful financial tuition as being able to teach your kids to save, spend and give. Although this sounds good, in isolation it is more romantic than practical when trying to navigate the new world above the age of 10! For example, most books talk about compound interest, which is great when we have great interest rates, but when savings rates are at historical lows and negative interest rates are in vogue internationally (which is when you have to pay the bank to take your money, not the other way around), compound interest seems less exciting or relevant. But understanding compound interest in reverse, to save money on a mortgage—well, that *is* worthy of discussion.

As the job landscape shifts, more of our kids will become self-employed and start their adulthood in debt. They are fighting a different type of financial war, and the weapons being passed down are at times out of date, or if not outdated, then not passed on with the right instructions to use them successfully.

Many of us prefer to keep our kids in the dark and avoid discussing socio-economic status because we feel kids don't notice class differences until they are teenagers. But very young children have a basic sense of what the words rich and poor mean.

American psychology professor Patricia G. Ramsey showed a group of three-year-olds a series of photographs which clearly distinguished between the 'haves' and 'have-nots' in each photo. Only half of the three-year-olds thought that the rich and poor people depicted would be friends.

Other research has shown that from as early as six, 'scores' are kept on which kids have what sorts of possessions and children begin to make judgements accordingly. By 11 or so, they are beginning to assume that social class is related to ambition or lack thereof (which as we know as adults isn't always true). From 14, they begin to wonder whether there is a larger economic system at work that may constrain movement between socio-economic classes.

The risk is that our kids can be jumping to big conclusions about differences which are not necessarily the right ones, especially if we are not engaging them in conversation along the way. We all know that by 17 they think they see how wrong the world is and how differently they would do things. Some school-leavers look at their parents with respect because of what they have achieved in their lifetime; many do not. This might be because the parents haven't achieved much, or have chosen not to share what has been achieved, or the kids don't have enough respect for their parents, or a combination of all of the above.

One of the lessons you need to teach your kids is that 'poor' is when you do not have enough money left at the end of the month. Most Kiwis, even middle- and upper-income earners, are poor.

POOR (ADJECTIVE)

When you have too much month left at the end of your money.

CHAPTER 2
FINDING A
SOLUTION

I am a chartered accountant with a Master's degree in tax. As I said earlier, I come from parents who are savers, yet I am a shopper. I love good food, a tidy house and family holidays. This usually translates to me spending more than I should on groceries, a cleaner and travel.

I am married to a Maori Scotsman. He is tight with money on everything, except for his art supplies and Xbox games. He works in advertising. His job is to get people to spend their discretionary dollar, while I fight for them to save it. If we weren't so shattered by the time we got home each night we might have some heated debates. But we are, so we don't!

I graduated from the University of Auckland in 1998, and then worked at KPMG for a time. My husband and I had a combined income of $32,000. We thought we were doing fine.

Fast-forward a few years and we were earning much more than our starting salaries, but this increase hadn't translated to any great financial progress.

We were earning good money, but we were also spending good money. We had more money coming in and just as much money going out. Our lifestyle cost more, which required us to work harder to maintain our new financial equilibrium. I never thought that we were bad with our money or that there were any obvious over-indulgences we could curb, however.

As our incomes increased, it became easier to spend without thought. On reflection, the more money we earned, the less we cared about money. It was almost like having plenty of money gave us permission to not worry about it, instead of doing the smartest thing with it. Fundamentally I felt that because we worked hard, we should be able to enjoy the fruits of our labours. I still hold this view, but in a slightly different form.

We never argued about money, as we were both apathetic when it came to our finances. We just didn't care enough. I managed the money, if you could call it 'manage'. Basically, I paid the bills and made sure that both of us could do what we needed or wanted to do because the money was always there. If it wasn't there, and I couldn't do what I wanted, maybe I would have cared more and maybe we would have argued.

Neither of us tended to use credit cards. We lived well pay-day to pay-day, but would run dry at the end of the pay cycle. There would be the occasional month that we might resort to our credit cards because of one-off costs. If I was to describe our situation I would say we were floating, but comfortable.

It is against this backdrop that we decided to buy our first home, for $350,000. We needed a mortgage of $300,000. We did what everyone does: we played the banks off against each other to get the best interest rate. We did get a good rate, but the interest saving achieved was comparably low, translating to an overall interest saving of $20,000 out of the $890,000 we were going to pay back to the bank over the life of the loan. It wasn't an insignificant saving, but comparatively small when we were looking down the barrel of $490,000 in interest obligations that we were going to pay to the bank over the next 30 years.

For some reason, I became fixated on how I could lower this interest cost. (This was obviously before I had children, when I had some mental capacity to 'wonder'!) I kind of understood that compound interest was making the amount so high, but I didn't really understand how compound interest worked, nor did I have an appreciation of how to reduce it.

In its simplest form, I recognised that the longer I had the mortgage with the bank the more money I would pay to the bank in interest. On a conceptual level, it was clear to me that to save myself paying so much interest, I would have to repay the loan faster. But I did not want to compromise my lifestyle to achieve this outcome. I felt that we worked hard and I wanted to enjoy what we earned. Equally, I acknowledged that the concepts of repaying my mortgage faster and living a life I enjoyed were not necessarily mutually exclusive; however, it would require a precise point of balance if I was to achieve both.

I wanted to understand how I could optimise the structure of my mortgage in order to repay it as quickly as possible. It was at this point that I reached out to Dr Jamie Sneddon, then a mathematics tutor at the University of Auckland. I met with Sneddon over the coming months, and after a few pages of calculus we found we had written a formula for structuring debt to repay it as fast as your circumstances allow, while also living the lifestyle you enjoy. I remember thinking: finally, a practical application of calculus! In any case, I call this 'Mortgage Optimisation', and I have since patented this formula. Working at its best, it can save more than the original mortgage amount in interest costs.

The formula assumes that you will have some money left over at the end of each week, month or year that can be used to repay your debt faster. This seemed reasonable. However, when trying to apply the formula to my own personal situation, I soon realised that, despite earning the most we had ever earned, we had no money left at the end of the month. So even though I had a powerful formula for debt reduction, it was of no value until I found out where my money was going and why I was not in control of it.

This is where it got interesting. Being an accountant, I helped my clients to manage their money. I could write a budget, I could colour-code it, but when it came to sticking to it, I couldn't do it. I could for a bit, but beyond that I lost interest.

While I don't tend to readily compare myself with others (again, who can be bothered?), I sought out friends and colleagues to determine if they had a similar financial landscape. Reassuringly, or disturbingly (depending on which way you view it), I found my husband and I were not alone. I was financially literate, yet struggling to make financial progress. I knew what I needed to do, but my own behaviour undermined my capability. I thought it was crazy that my psychology of spending had a bigger outcome than my income level. But there it was.

Personally, I am and always will be a shopper. Telling me to go without does not motivate me. I *can* go without, I just choose not to. However, if you were to give me a valid reason why I should try, then I will. The reasons behind this are interesting, but in short, in absence of a reason not to, then I am more likely to spend than save. I don't spend with abandon, but if I have the option of spending money or not, I will usually opt to spend because I find it easier.

For the record, shoppers are not irrational people—we just need a reason not to shop, as we are predisposed to spend or share money rather than to save it. Being time-poor or taking my kids shopping with me are two effective ways of stopping me spending money. Lack of time, or the process being generally unpleasant, make for effective deterrents.

For me, in this instance the reason to do things smarter was the idea of paying $490,000 in interest to the bank over the life of our loan. Quite simply, I didn't want to pay the bank this money! I appreciated them lending it to me, but I felt the amount I had to repay in exchange was completely over the top, bordering on criminal. Albert Einstein is said to have said, 'Compound interest is the eighth wonder of the world. He who understands it, earns it . . . he who doesn't, pays it.' All I can say to this is that the banks understand this wonder very well and use it to their advantage (which is entirely their prerogative, because without them I wouldn't have been able to buy the property).

Because I also didn't want to lose my home, the only way I was going to pay less was to pay my mortgage off faster. The question was, how could I do this and still be happy with my life? Although I am a shopper, I am not stupid, nor am I financially illiterate. I respond well to impartial and qualified, intelligent advice. I respond even better to results.

In my research, I learned that, as soon as you start out on any financial journey, life throws you curve balls and you need to learn how to navigate around them. I learned that our expenses were seldom consistent from month to month, that our spending was up and down from month to month, and that a normal budget doesn't easily reflect that because of its rigidity, which made it difficult to easily depict or interpret progress. I learned that what motivated me did not motivate my husband. I learned we each had different spending needs. I learned that unless I am accountable to someone, then I am off on a tangent. The busier I was, the more accountable I needed to be. I learned that I had a different money personality and risk profile than my husband and that this played out in different settings, with us each frustrating the other at times.

But slowly, I determined a way to keep us on track. I started to understand our financial pressure points and how to overcome them . . . and quickly momentum built. Our journey to being mortgage-free started with us starting. Then we had to train, to sharpen our financial skills, and put to use what we were learning, by practising.

As we got busier, I found I needed someone to keep me accountable. Not because I didn't know what I needed to do—I knew it, I just struggled to do it consistently. I needed someone to help keep my 'eyes on the prize', to motivate me to keep going. Despite my husband trying, it wasn't going to be him, as I wasn't interested in being accountable to him with my spending. (In fact, I would go so far as to say that this arrangement might be the single fastest way to destroy a good relationship, which is probably why financial stress and communication are rated among the top contributors to divorce.)

When talking to my friends and peers, it seemed I was not alone. The more people I shared my story with, the more fascinated people became. I talked about money and my experience with it openly and honestly, and shared the lessons I had learned. People got on board with me. I was able to keep testing and fine-tuning the different paths people needed to take depending on their starting point, money personality, end goal and time remaining to get there.

Early on, I formed the company enableMe to help people get in control of their finances. Soon we described ourselves as Financial Personal Trainers. We wanted to help our clients get ahead faster, by providing a constructive solution for those who want to become financially successful, irrespective of their money personality, gender, wealth or age.

HELPING PEOPLE BECOME MORTGAGE-FREE

Money is an emotional topic. Uncovering a person's money personality can be a sensitive path to go down. It is intrinsically linked to your sense of self-worth and self-esteem, yet few of the tools available talk about this honestly, dealing with the science of getting ahead and not the behaviours behind it. There is an assumption that if you spend less than you earn, you will be fine. But in my case, that is like telling someone who has a sluggish metabolism (also known as a penchant for shopping) to exercise more and eat less. I mean, I get it, but who is going to help me to do that, because it certainly doesn't come easy to me over the long term.

At enableMe, we are a team of chartered accountants and financial advisors working with our clients to get them ahead faster. We have 10 offices throughout New Zealand, and have worked with clients all around the world. We have now worked with more than 6000 clients and have a success rate of more than 90 per cent (although this rate is likely skewed by the fact that people work with us because they want to get ahead faster, and are ready in themselves to do things better).

In my role as CEO of this company, I have been exposed to

many varied client situations. The demographics vary considerably. Income levels range from $50,000 to $2,000,000 per annum. Some clients have mortgages, some don't. Some are starting out financially, others are nearing the end of their working life. Some client couples are financially compatible, many are not; some are self-employed, more are employed. The consistent theme is that they all want to be doing better than they currently are, and all are ready to be held accountable to a result. We have helped many clients get in control of their money, kill their mortgages, improve their business performance, reconnect with their spouse and sort their retirement. That said, what has astounded me is the number of clients who have adult children who are not financially independent, which in turn is impacting on the parents' ability to reach their financial goals—which is what led me to write this book.

We work with some clients for a year, most for longer. The typical client journey starts with an initial meeting to determine their current situation: where they are at, and whether they are on track to achieve their financial goals. We then determine if there are inefficiencies in their situation (whether they fritter their money, have a plan against which they are monitoring their performance, are paying too much in tax or interest, or simply need a strategy). We then model their scenario based on either a tweak or an overhaul of their current situation. If this shows we can get them to their goals faster, and the results are compelling, the client usually opts to work with us. We then set out a game plan, put the right framework in place and start moving forward. Most people fritter money; if they have a mortgage it is probably set up incorrectly; if they are self-employed the levels of inefficiencies are greater again. In any case, we help them capture the frittered money and push them forward, faster.

Over the space of time we get them mortgage-free and help them progress towards retirement.

I remember when we launched the enableMe Mortgage Free Club™, four years after launching enableMe. Like many of our enableMe products, we launched it because a client had reached that status and was now ready for the next challenge. I still remember my first client who became mortgage-free. It was so exciting! On reflection, I am not sure who was more excited, me or the client! It was through consistent efforts in all areas that they achieved this result—not because the universe wished it, but because they wanted it and were prepared to fight for it, despite the inconsistencies of life and family.

Paying off your mortgage is the first big step towards becoming financially independent. With this client, much like myself when I paid off my mortgage, all that was needed from that point on was for them to save the money that they had previously been paying to the bank. In fact, even if this client just left those savings in the bank, and didn't invest them, the rate at which the savings would grow (through more saving, as opposed to interest earned) meant they would have accumulated enough by retirement age to fund their retirement. All that was needed in their case was to redirect their annual cash surplus, which used to be channelled into the mortgage, into a savings account.

Simple. It makes sense, but do you think our mortgage-free clients could save at the rate they were paying off debt? No. In most instances, there appeared to be some kind of force field between them and their savings account. I don't know why some people find it easier to pay off debt than to save; all I know is that it just is, and more so if you are a shopper, where the force field appears stronger.

TRYING TO SUCCEED

My team and I have developed tools to overcome these types of challenges. However, as I said above, one of the setbacks that I struggled to deal with was the adult children of my clients who were not as financially independent as they should have been, given their age and stage of life.

We have often been taken aback by how overtly generous our clients can be, often giving money they barely have to kids who need it less than the parents do. I have been astounded by how often people had adult children living at home and not paying board. I tended to leave these areas alone, due to the sensitivity around them. I usually wasn't forced to take a more direct approach if there were plenty of other things we could improve first. However, once all the other areas had been tidied up, I would find myself being forced to tackle the lack of financial autonomy of my clients' children, given that it was starting to derail my best-laid retirement plans for them. These are dangerous waters to swim in, and I would only do so if I considered it absolutely necessary to confront the situation head on.

Also, I saw that many of our clients were financially smart in their day job, and earned good money, but this was not enough in isolation to create strong financial results. Two generations ago it would have been. More and more clients were coming through with student loans which proved challenging when buying their first home—a task which already felt nigh on impossible.

For example, a couple of years ago, a couple came to me (let's call them Sally and Tom) who on paper seemed to have done things right—or, more accurately, they hadn't done anything obviously wrong—when it came to their finances. Both Sally and Tom were university trained and working in their chosen fields. Both were on good incomes and had a clear history of both living within their means and saving. They had two primary-school-aged children.

Sally was currently between jobs, but was employable. They had done their OE and had almost paid off their student loans. They were saving well, which made them better off than most. But they had still not saved enough to get on to the property ladder, and their rate of saving was not enough to keep up with the property market.

They felt there was nothing obvious that they were doing wrong. Sure, there were some things they could do better, but if you were to compare them to others at the same stage in life, they were tracking slightly above average.

When they came in for their first meeting, Sally cried. She said she felt hopeless and that they would never have what they wanted, which was a house for her kids to grow up in. I told her that her kids wouldn't care what property they grew up in, provided the family unit is content, which made her cry more. She subtly blamed Tom for not earning enough, which in my view was a bit rough given he was at the top earning level for his field, and she was also projecting her own desire for a home on to her kids. But that was not really the point. She was frustrated and fatigued by their lack of progress towards her goal of owning a home.

I listened. I empathised with them. It was possible to fix their situation, but we had to think creatively because their traditional approach to getting ahead was not actually getting them ahead, and while they were already good at saving, they had to be better.

I wanted to get a deeper understanding of what had happened in the previous 10 years, to get a better feel of why they were in their current position. All that could be said was that there were a few missteps—nothing outrageous, but still some setbacks.

The problem, though, as is the case with many middle-income families, is that there is no tolerance or buffer for getting it wrong. They had had a shot at getting it right and they did better than most, but it was still not enough to change their outcome. They had started a fraction too late, had kids a fraction too early, and this was making it harder and harder to keep up and get ahead.

This scenario isn't new. A lot of my clients are like this when they first start working with me. Disturbingly, I am seeing more and more younger clients (late twenties to early thirties) who want to get ahead, but are instead going nowhere fast.

But Tom and Sally's story bugged me. It bugged me because they were already trying hard, but effort in isolation was not enough. They earned good money, but this wasn't enough. There will always be people who don't try, and I have no sympathy for their lack of results, but if you try and you don't succeed, contrary to the cliché 'pick yourself up and try again', when it comes to money, that usually doesn't work. I knew that if they kept trying and kept coming up short, they would either be miserable or divorce (and still possibly be miserable). That was the truth. A lack of progress plays out somewhere, eventually.

Tom and Sally were drawing the wrong conclusions as to why they were where they were, blaming the wrong things and getting more and more jaded with every month that went by. Two things struck me: firstly, that they were already doing better than average, which normally means you can have a good innings, but for them being better than most still translated to financial idleness. Secondly, they were too young to be this jaded. I felt the system had let them down.

(You will be pleased to know that we managed to get them into their first home within 12 months, but it took some drastic measures, and that isn't the point of this story.)

Surely there had to be a better way—a way of helping our young people succeed, and in exchange helping their parents reach a comfortable retirement without having dependent adult children?

FINDING A SOLUTION

So I had mature clients not achieving their retirement objectives because they were too generous with their kids, and parents of teenagers conditioning their children to become dependent, letting them live in a world disconnected from reality (although in keeping with their peers). I had 30-somethings seemingly having taken the right course but feeling disillusioned around money and their lack of progress. I had smart people earning good money who, if left to their own devices, would stand still because the tide was no longer strong enough to push them forward. Then I looked at my own children and felt nervous about how entitled they seemed to be, as well as their natural tendencies around money. Society is making it harder to get ahead, and today's kids are less equipped for financial reality than their parents.

All these factors pointed to the need to do something about this problem, and I toyed with the idea of writing a book. But it felt too hard, so like a lot of things that are too hard, it went into the 'I'll get back to that later' pile.

Then, two things happened that pushed the problem to the top of my 'let's sort this once and for all' pile.

Firstly, I hired two millennials to work for enableMe: Ellen and Natalie. They are both very capable young ladies, born into the era whose mantra is 'you only live once'. I genuinely liked and rated them both, and spent many a lunchtime debating different issues with them. Boy oh boy, do they see the world differently to me! I was interested in their view of money: whether they had financial goals, whether they were living at home, whether they had a student loan, and whether they cared? I also reached out to their parents to understand the extent to which they were prepared to support them to become financially independent, if at all. The more I learned, the more disturbed I became. I concluded that the whole system had lost its way.

Then my seven-year-old son told me that he was happy to forfeit his pocket money because he didn't want to do his chores anymore. I think the exact conversation went along the lines of:

Me: Cam, you need to make your bed, can you please turn the TV off and do it?

Cam: I don't want to.

Me: Whether you want to or not is irrelevant. It's part of your chores.

Cam: I don't want to do chores. I'm happy to go without my pocket money.

Me: It's not up for debate. We all do chores, so please go and do what you have been told to do.

Cut to: TV being turned off, Cameron being marched to his bedroom and told not to come out until his bed is made.

Cam: Mummmmmmm!

Cameron comes out of his room 30 minutes later, with the bed still unmade but his Lego Ninjago set rebuilt. Cameron is sent back to his room to make his bed.

Cameron coaxes his little sister into his room and tells her he will let her play with his toys if she makes his bed.

Madison makes Cam's bed.

Cameron comes out of his room and declares his bed is made and he would like his pocket money now.

Time taken: 45 minutes.

Time it would have taken me: 2 minutes.

Times I debated just making the bed myself: three.

Mental exhaustion: Moderate.

Rating of parenting: Too tired to think.

What we conclude from this is that not only is my son a hustler, but the pocket-money system is flawed (possibly in conjunction with my parenting style).

The society we have created is broken. It is now not enough to work hard anymore. It's not enough for my generation, let alone the generations after me. We must work *smart*. Working smart still implies you work hard (contrary to a millennial's interpretation of that point), but the output needs to be bigger for every amount of input. If you make the wrong turn, it could take years to sort it out, and the likelihood of you owning a home and funding your retirement no longer go hand in hand.

Faced with this realisation, I decided that I needed to understand the problem better so I could create a formula of success to overcome it. So, over the last two years, I have set about working with the children of my clients to understand what they know about money, and what they don't know; where they learned their financial lessons and how they were taught. I have worked to understand their trigger points, weaknesses and opportunities. I have worked with parents and their kids together to better understand their family dynamics around money and identify what money conversations are being had, and what is missing. More importantly, I have looked at what conversations aren't being *heard* because they are being delivered by the wrong person, at the wrong time or in the wrong manner.

Separate to this, I have interviewed hundreds of children outside of my enableMe 'family', from Years 10–13 and school-leavers. I have interviewed millennials, careers advisors, family therapists, parenting coaches and child psychologists, retired bankers, financial advisors and even my own parents. I have spoken to university lecturers, design thinkers and plain old parents.

I have been disturbed and excited by some of my findings, which I will share with you in this book. This book is not designed to be parenting advice. This is financial advice for you as a parent. Franklin D. Roosevelt said it best: 'We cannot always build the future for our youth, but we can build our youth for the future.'

What we know is that it is getting harder for each generation to get ahead. Financial success is not a rite of passage. Traditional means of getting ahead will now only get you so far. We need our kids to be better equipped to deal with the changing landscape.

As a parent, I believe that all we want for our kids is for them to be happy and have a successful life. We want our kids to thrive in spite of the winds of change. We know that we are entering uncertain times, but we need to show our kids how to succeed regardless. To be the opposite of fragile. Trader-turned-author Nassim Nicholas Taleb, who has been referred to as a 'superhero of the mind', explains in his book *Antifragile* that some things benefit from shocks. They thrive and grow when exposed to volatility, randomness, risk and uncertainty. He calls these things the opposite of fragile and has coined the term antifragile to describe this phenomenon. He explains that antifragile is beyond resilience, as resilience resists shocks and stays the same. Antifragile gets better.

This is where it gets interesting. I believe the current education system is creating fragile adults, when to survive we need to be antifragile. If we deprive our kids of randomness, a degree of volatility (not in terms of temperament) and stressors, we harm them, weakening their ability to survive and thrive.

To illustrate this, if you spent a year in bed, it would lead to muscle atrophy, as your body and its complex internal system is weakened when deprived of exercise. As Taleb writes: 'This is the tragedy of modernity: as with the neurotically overprotective parents, those trying to help are often hurting us most. The process of discovery depends on antifragile thinking, being able to tolerate life's frustrations and setbacks, which you do not get from formal education.'

I believe, as a financial advisor and Financial Personal Trainer, that there is an onus on all parents to equip their children with the financial reality of what they will face in life, so that they can devise the right strategy and move forward with confidence. For some parents, this will mean that they must face their own financial reality first.

This is more important than ever before, as our children face unprecedented financial and cultural challenges. The objective of this book is to shed some light upon the unspoken truths around money, and provide some framework around fixing the problem. Most importantly, I want you to feel empowered and equipped to give your kids the head-start they need to thrive in life.

CHAPTER 3
HOW DO OUR KIDS LEARN TO MANAGE MONEY?

The grim reality is that most don't. And most adults learn about money as the result of their own successes and failures.

Research shows that adults are failing with money because of the money habits they developed as children. CNN reported on a study of college students and concluded that most of the ideas we have about kids and money are wrong. For example, one of the similarities among students who demonstrated good financial skills was that 'nearly all said their parents had got them into the habit of saving as young children', suggesting that saving is a behaviour that comes from experience, not knowledge. Some financial experts suggest personal finance is 80 per cent behaviour and 20 per cent knowledge—which is probably true, as evidenced by an entirely new discipline being created at universities in the last few decades called behavioural economics.

As we know, kids observe their parents' behaviour irrespective of whether the parent shares any teaching to accompany it. However, if the parents' money management skills are not what they would like them to be, cause conflict between parents, or are unnecessarily complex, it is hard for their children to gain any real insights.

To make matters worse, kids today have more money to spend and develop financial styles at a younger age than ever. And most parents don't deal with their kids' money management problems until their children are adults. By then, these problems can be both costly and emotionally charged.

The only way kids will learn to manage their money is through their own experience and the guidance you, as parents, give them. In other words, kids learn from trial and error and role models just like the rest of us. And if they can't learn as children, the price of adult mistakes can be great in terms of money and relationships.

YOU CAN'T FATTEN A THOROUGHBRED

We are all programmed a certain way. Some things are easier for some people, and harder for others. Some of us have a fast metabolism. Some of us don't. (Don't I know it!) The old saying 'you can't fatten a thoroughbred' speaks to this, acknowledging that some of us seem predestined for an outcome even if we try to sabotage that outcome with our own efforts (or lack thereof).

Some people will find financial success easier to achieve than others. But just because you are predisposed somehow does not predetermine your end—it simply gives you a head-start. Just because you start well, or you feel advantaged, you are not guaranteed a result. An advantage, if acknowledged but not utilised, will work against you, because it creates complacency. And complacency is enemy number one of financial success.

We often see this play out in life and business. The big guy gets overtaken by the little guy. David and Goliath, Microsoft and Apple, the tortoise and the hare. The characteristics of the little guy are the same every time. To succeed, you have to understand what you bring to the table—and understand what you don't. Develop skills. Understand your kryptonite. Find your sun (see chapter 1). If complacency is the kryptonite, then persistency is the sun. Our kryptonite cancels out any financial gains we make and puts us squarely on the back foot. Some of us don't have any obvious kryptonite, but we also don't have any obvious edge, which means we too are starting on the back foot. Getting ahead is not supposed to be easy, but life can make it harder than it needs to be. Parents usually make it harder again.

There are two types of parents: parents who know their children have a financial advantage and those who know they don't. Both sets of children will face particular obstacles as they grow up. Chance will always be a factor. Some people will be blessed, others won't. Some will put their faith in the universe or the laws of attraction. While I acknowledge such laws might exist, I prefer to take steps to ensure successful results outside of the things I can't control.

THE KEYS TO SUCCESS

Many a financial book will tell you simply to spend less than you earn. Good practical advice that you can't fault. But for most of us, even if we do this or have been lucky enough to be genetically programmed to be a natural saver (the financial version of a thoroughbred), this doesn't ensure success. But it will help. Some will find it easier to understand wealth principles than others. Some start off well, but have a financial setback, and some don't bother to even start.

To increase your chances of succeeding at anything, you need to learn the rules of the game. If you think you are disadvantaged, then maybe you are. But every success story has disadvantage sprinkled throughout it. The difference is that the challenge is not what defines them, but the successful outcome.

If you are not a saver, own it. If you are a shopper, own it. We have to diagnose ourselves accurately if we are to learn to combat our weaknesses, leverage off our strengths and drive a result. The universe owes you nothing. Don't bother following your dreams. Chase them.

Financial success is not a rite of passage. It is not an entitlement and you cannot will it to happen. Most of us have to 'drive' an outcome, as being passive will not cut it.

HOW A CHILD'S RELATIONSHIP WITH MONEY DEVELOPS

There are four main factors at play here:
- genetics
- money personality
- ability to delay gratification, and
- confidence with money.

Money personalities are usually determined early on, influenced by genetics, and aside from a 'financial Mac truck' event—where you get completely mown down—usually stay the same throughout life. Our ability to delay gratification starts with the brain but is a skill that can be nurtured. As your understanding and mastery of money increases, so too does your competence. With competence comes mastery, and financial confidence develops.

Genetics

A new study of twins has found that one-third of our behaviour when it comes to money is influenced by our genetics, rather than being our natural choice. People are genetically predisposed to save or spend the money they have, regardless of their wealth, gender or upbringing.

Some of us are genetically programmed to behave in a certain way when it comes to money. We are hard-wired. This is not to say you cannot overcome this tendency, because you can. But it needs to be actively overcome, requiring a degree of effort or discipline.

George Loewenstein, a professor of economics and psychology at Carnegie Mellon University in Australia, and his colleagues surveyed more than 13,000 people, beginning back in 2004. Respondents reported how their actual spending diverged from their desired spending habits. From this Loewenstein's team was able to get a more accurate picture of how many people lie at the extreme edges of the spectrum, either being spendthrifts (extreme shoppers) or tightwads (miserly savers).

Further studies used brain-scanning techniques to monitor blood flow to the areas in the brain activated when a subject was presented with an item of desire, and then its price tag or cost. This further highlighted the distinguishing factors of extreme money personalities, as it related to their brain activity.

Researchers would first show the study subject a product. If they liked it, the reward centres of the brain would light up. Then researchers would show the subject the product's price. This then triggered an area of the brain that acts as a 'handbrake'. In the tightwad or saver subjects, brain activity in the handbrake region was more pronounced when they viewed the price.

These scanning studies show that an area of the brain, called the nucleus accumbens, 'lights up' when people think about things that have a reward attached. When this 'gas pedal' is activated, dopamine is released and the brain benefits from a natural high. Dopamine is a compound in the brain that helps control its reward and pleasure centres, and is a precursor to adrenaline. It helps regulate movement and emotional responses to stimuli, and it enables us not only to recognise rewards, but to take action and start to move towards them.

In consumer behaviours, there are certain buying decisions that trigger this part of the brain. Anything that promises some sort of emotional reward can trigger these circuits. We start envisioning what possession of the object would be like: the taste of a meal, the excitement of a holiday, the joy of a new home or, in Loewenstein's example, the reward used was the simple indulgence of a piece of chocolate.

Thankfully, our brain is not only driven by reward. We have a braking system that helps regulate the nucleus accumbens. Again, brain scanning has identified a small section of the brain called the anterior insula as one of the structures serving this role. The insula is the angst centre of our brain. Through the release of noradrenaline and other neurochemicals, it creates a sense of gnawing anxiety that causes us to slow down and tread carefully. In extreme cases, it can even evoke disgust. The findings suggest that the emotional pain or anxiety of having to pay for an item works to keep our pleasure-seeking in check.

In some people, the researchers think, this mental anguish

is so strong that it overrides rational deliberation; these people are tightwads, and they don't buy things even when they know they should.

For a spendthrift (shopaholic), the pain of throwing money around does not register in the brain like it does for other people. They experience little to no pain when spending money, and therefore part with their money more easily. Spending by credit card acts to distance the pain and the cost of the item being bought from the pleasure of enjoying it now, and can be an effective technique to overcome the handbrake message being sent by the brain.

What this research shows is that some of us are genetically more likely to behave a certain way when it comes to money. For shoppers this is a bit of a concern, because this means that your wiring is not to your financial advantage. Delayed gratification does not come as easily to the shopper as it does the saver (see later in this chapter for more on this). Your anterior insula is off on holiday, or at the very least not firing on all cylinders. So you are going to have to consciously train your brain to recognise that forgoing pleasure now can bring a greater pay-off later.

As a parent, you might encourage your kids to delay spending in order to buy something bigger and of better quality, rather than succumbing to the notion of buying cheap things more frequently. It works with homework, too: doing homework tonight can create better grades next month. You are teaching your kids to develop willpower and patience through practice.

Neuroeconomist Paul Zak of Claremont Graduate University in California claims that it is possible to increase the number or strength of the calming signals your brain produces, to delay impulsiveness, but this skill needs to be learned, because genetically not all brains are pre-set this way.

As an extension of his research, he further comments that when 'people are happier and have greater social support' they save more. The happier you are, the more patient you can be and 'the more likely we will make decisions that are better for us', claims Zak.

This rings true to me, because in my day job, I help shoppers achieve their financial goals, despite their natural tendencies. Accountability and support are precursors to a better result with regard to most things in life, but especially with the things that you find hard to do.

Money personalities

In addition to the education you give your children around money, you need to take time to determine their money personality, as this will heavily influence their relationship with money. When trying to diagnose human personality, psychologists focus on the measurement of traits: habitual patterns of behaviour, thought and emotion. Unlike more transient states of mind, personality traits are thought to be fairly stable over time, differ between individuals and influence people's behaviour.

Some traits can be measured on a spectrum (for example, extraversion versus introversion), while other traits you either have or you don't, there is no in-between. Psychologists break down the various traits into five key areas: openness, conscientiousness, extraversion, agreeableness and neuroticism. They define personality as the individual differences in the way people tend to think, feel and behave. Our personality is the sum of our habitual patterns of behaviour.

Your money personality works the same way. It is the series of traits that come together to make your relationship with money unique to you. Theories differ as to how many money personality traits there are, although most agree that they can be slotted into two broad categories—your cash flow and your strategic personality—with a weighting then given to which of the two categories is more dominant in influencing your financial behaviour.

Your money personality is twofold, and covers both your cash flow and strategic tendencies. When it comes to money, most of us will have a natural tendency to either spend or save, and to be strategically adventurous or risk-averse, although some people fall in the middle.

The three cash flow personalities are Shopper, Saver and Plodder. The strategic personalities—how much we are prepared to plan and take on risk—are: Adventurer (risk-taker), Safe-keeper (consistent) or Dreamer (whatever goes).

Cash flow personality	Strategic personality
Shopper	Adventurer (risk-taker/daredevil/outgoing)
Saver	Safe-keeper (safety warden/worrier)
Plodder	Dreamer (no plan/laid-back)

Your money personality has nothing to do with your budget, your net worth, level of debt or retirement savings balance. It is not linked to your level of financial literacy or gender. Financially literate people can have trouble sticking to a budget. In fact, those who manage money as part of their day-to-day job (accountants, managers, CEOs, etc.) tend to be terrible with money in their personal life. They get it, they can do it as part of their job, but in their own time, it is not a priority. It's almost as if we have an allergic reaction to it, or get decision fatigue, because financial decisions fill so much of our week already.

There is no correlation between being rational in your everyday life and being rational with money. The two points are not interdependent. Builders don't finish their homes, accountants are late filing their own tax returns and the mechanic's car still needs to be fixed. Knowing and doing are two very different things.

Each personality has its strengths and its challenges. Each of them can help you make great financial decisions, and each has the potential to get you into financial trouble. There is no right or wrong personality. But understanding your personality helps you understand your perspective on how you deal with money. In understanding the cons of each personality trait, you can better identify the tools you need or the skills that must be learned to mitigate against the risks of your financial tendencies.

Some people can identify their personality without too much prodding. Some of us have some tendencies across the board. If you can't easily identify your spending habit, ask your partner or a friend—they don't usually pull any punches.

When I interview my clients, I ask them to describe their own money personality and their partner's. I then ask their partner to answer the same question. Our clients tend to be more forthright when diagnosing their partner than themselves. As parents, you need to be aware of this when diagnosing your children's personalities.

Knowing your own money personality as a parent can also help you figure out why you become frustrated, angry, controlling or anxious in different money situations. Your money personality is as much a part of you as your metabolism. Embrace your personality and start paying attention to the areas in which it affects your life. The more you know about how you view money, the better equipped you are to overcome your challenges.

Cash flow personalities

Shoppers

As an adult, shoppers find it easier to spend money than to save. They are neither stupid nor irrational, but need a reason to not spend, as opposed to a reason to spend. They can derive emotional satisfaction from spending money. They like to shop and are usually good at it.

Some spend little amounts often. Others can be quite tight on a day-to-day basis, but when they find something they really want, they will buy it. I would call the latter person a controlled or bargain shopper, but a shopper nonetheless.

Some will shop because they are feeling good, but many shop because they simply do not have a reason not to. Not finding it easy to save merely means you have not been given a reason compelling enough to stop spending.

Subcategories of the shopper include the comfort shopper and the binger. I am probably a comfort shopper (and eater, truth be told). A comfort shopper spends money as a way of celebration or distraction. If they are happy they spend money, or if they are sad or feeling out of control then they spend money. The extreme comfort shopper does both. The binger can be quite controlled for a while, but when the occasion calls for it, they can shop like the best of them. Bingers can budget for a time, and then they blow out.

Not everyone is a shopper all the time, but overall shoppers find it easier to spend money than to save it. Shoppers live in the moment and can be impulsive and sometimes impatient. On the plus side, shoppers are big-hearted and tend to be generous. They find it harder to stick to a budget than a saver does.

Signs your child might be a shopper:
- They crave instant gratification, want things now, not

later, and can be impulsive in their spending. They can be relentless in their 'gimmes' in the checkout line. They don't really care what they get, just that they get something.

- They can be impulsive with any money received, wanting to buy something quickly. They don't always delineate between wants and needs, and both come across as equally important.

- There seems to be little connection between work ethic and money personality, although most spenders that I have met tend to work hard, sometimes to enable them to spend harder! This starts to present itself with teenagers who are happy to work and earn money, but only so they can spend it, so they are often broke.

- Shoppers tend to be generous and enjoy buying things for other people as much as for themselves. Because they are often looking for new things, they don't always value what they have, neglecting it and not caring for it as some other children (namely savers) might.

Savers

Savers derive more satisfaction from saving than spending. They are not necessarily of Scottish decent (sorry for the racial profiling), but people from certain cultural backgrounds do have stronger tendencies in this area, due to their history. (The same applies to people brought up in the Depression, who are less likely to be shoppers.) They are happy to go without or delay a purchase and can more readily resist temptation.

Savers will rarely buy impulsively. They will turn the lights off when they leave the room, reuse plastic bags and prefer to keep something, even if it is broken, rather than throw it away.

Savers can have hoarder tendencies. They are happy to recycle and buy second-hand rather than new. If they don't have an immediate use for something, they will store it until they need it.

My husband is a saver. At times it is a helpful calming mechanism to my penchant for spending, but at other times I feel I am living with a hoarder.

(Random tip: Never throw out any possessions of a saver—even if they have never used them and are unlikely to ever use them. Even if their hoarder tendencies are driving you crazy! Invest in storage.)

Not all savers save in the same way. Not every saver objects to buying something new. Some wear designer clothes, but they buy them at a discount. Some drive nice cars, and go on great holidays. The difference between a saver and a shopper is that the saver is more likely to save before spending the money, often paying for things in cash and spending more consciously, rather than relying on credit.

Savers are usually more organised with their finances. The most extreme will save at someone else's expense—a trait I deplore. Within every circle of friends, there is always 'that friend' who is a little too tight or cheap.

Signs your child may be a saver:

- They love to collect things: rocks, sticks, bottle caps, marbles. They keep things in a safe place and value the littlest of trinkets. They don't spend as impulsively as spenders and enjoy getting a good deal.
- For some kids, spending money can create a sense of anxiousness or a change in demeanour. They would simply prefer to not spend their money. They consume things more slowly. For example, if they are given a lot of lollies at Christmas, a saver child is more likely to eat their chocolate more slowly than their spender sibling.

- Savers find it easier to set financial goals and are at an advantage over spenders. But with this advantage can come a lack of forward strategy, as they don't want to part with their money.
- While it might not be as obvious when your kids are young, a saver tends to have a good short-term or 'working' memory. This means that they are able to project themselves into the future and plan for it, which is a prerequisite of saving, as achieving a goal requires keeping it in mind.

Plodders

The plodder is not really a shopper or a saver. While not having any clear evidence of large or frequent spending patterns, a plodder doesn't have much to show for the fact that they are not spending money either—and they are usually financially frustrated by this.

Signs your child may be a plodder:

- They are not overly generous or excessive in their spending habits, and are sometimes aimless with their desires. I personally didn't show shopper tendencies until I started earning money, so it may be that the lack of consistent income is making it difficult to determine where a plodder child may be likely to end up.

Outliers

Within the three money personalities, there is a spectrum. For example, a shopper is someone who enjoys spending money. If they can't control this urge then they are considered a shopaholic or a spendthrift. Similarly, a saver is happy to go without, but some savers, again at the extreme, have physical difficulty in spending money—it pains them to do so. A study published in the *Journal of Consumer Research* in 2008 indicated that around 25 per cent of us are tightwads and 16 per cent are shopaholics. The majority (60 per cent) sits in the middle of the bell curve.

This study also showed that males were three times more likely to be tightwads than females (no great surprises there), who showed no bias towards either category. The use of a credit card was found to be a financial equaliser, as credit cards weaken impulse control, particularly for those who wouldn't normally be very careful with their money—whether male or female. Not having to give up anything tangible seemed to help cure tightwads of their affliction.

For spendthrifts, the medium of purchasing didn't really matter. That said, spendthrifts who used credit cards were three times more likely to have debt than tightwads who also swiped the plastic.

Income levels did not vary much between the two personalities, suggesting that spending decisions arose not from the size of one's bank balance, but from ingrained spending behaviours.

Strategic personalities

Once you have defined your kid's cash flow personality or tendencies, you need to ascertain what their strategic preference is. In *The 5 Money Conversations to Have with your Kids at Every Age and Stage*, authors Scott and Bethany Palmer spend some time going into the different risk personalities. While I agree with some of their observations, I don't agree with all of them. They make some interesting observations around risk types, but what impacts upon financial results, more than money personality, is a person's strategic tendency (not just their risk make-up).

In the current economic climate, and in keeping with future change and uncertainty, it is imperative that you identify your child's tendencies in this area as innate strengths and skills emerge. While their strategic personalities can have an equally positive or detrimental effect on your kids' financial futures, they will also reveal natural career clues.

Adventurers

The adventurer is the risk-taker, the financial daredevil. Where others might see risk, they tend to see opportunity.

I love risk-takers, because I am one. We are big-picture people. It's not that we don't appreciate the detail, it's just the detail doesn't excite us as much. We don't get hung up on the 'how' of the idea, instead we move, fast—whether it is a business opportunity, an investment or a property deal. We are looking for adventure and get excited by possibility. We create opportunity, we don't wait for it to arrive.

Scott and Bethany Palmer distinguish a financial adventurer as someone who is not afraid to make decisions, nor are they afraid to move fast. If it doesn't feel right, a risk-taker walks away. They accept that there will be some deals that go wrong. They are not afraid of failing. If we fail, we can fail fast, picking ourselves up quickly and moving on to the next thing.

We use intuition and our 'gut' as the deciding factor. If something doesn't feel right, we won't touch it. But if it has that special thing, that *je ne sais quoi*, we don't let go easily.

Risk-takers are not afraid to make decisions, and we are not afraid to make decisions fast. This approach can scare the living daylights out of someone who is not a risk-taker. We don't like feeling constrained and resent being held back. We tend to make a move forward even if we do not have the full backing of our team, because we believe in ourselves.

Our shortcomings are that we can be blinded by an idea, impatient to execute it and slow to compromise. For example, a risk-taker would book a holiday without researching it.

Signs your kid may be an adventurer:

- They tend to dream big and have big ideas. They naturally think outside of the box and tend to be fearless. They can make decisions easily. They know what they want and trust their intuition, acting on hunches. They can make friends quickly and can instinctively find something that connects them with someone to leverage a friendship from. They love to negotiate or trade. They love the new and are happy to live on the edge.

- Adventurers tend to be careless about details. They can make plans, but not all the detail is considered. At times, they can be perceived as insensitive, because they are on a mission and are not particularly interested in the views of people who are not on board with what they are trying to accomplish. They expose themselves, and can be hurt or misinterpreted at times.

- They see the possibility and not always the obstacles. But the daredevil is more likely to change the world than not. They have a greater likelihood of becoming entrepreneurs.

- The role of the parent is to help them navigate to their potential without leaving a trail of wreckage in their wake. To a financial adventurer, just because someone else hasn't done it, is not a reason why it can't be done. This can be exciting if someone is investing in you, and scary if you are married to them.

Safety wardens

The safety warden needs financial security and consistency. They are not boring, but they are predictable and prefer little to no risk. Safety wardens are happy to spend money, and will invest, but they want to make sure they are spending their money wisely and the safer the investment, the better.

Adventurers scare them, which can cause pressure in a relationship if their partner is one. Even if they believe in their partner, they may still struggle to accept the risk that the partner wants to undertake, which the adventurer typically interprets as not having faith in them.

Safety wardens want to know that the future is settled and safe. While gender is not a significant factor in risk personalities, I have a lot of older female clients who have ended long-standing relationships because they can no longer abide the risk tendencies or lack of action from their partner. They deem it safer to go it alone than to rely on someone else.

Safety wardens investigate and research. They are prepared to invest, but they do their homework. They do a *lot* of homework, sometimes to the point of paralysis. They are willing to sacrifice and are prepared for the worst. They tend to be more negative than positive about investments, sticking to the certainties rather than the possibilities, and making decisions out of fear. That said, safety wardens can make good partners because their careful planning and steady approach to money can help a couple avoid disaster.

Signs your kid may be a safety warden:

- They need clear expectations and want to know what is coming, what the rules are and how things may play out. They can be easily frustrated if insufficient detail is given. They like information and knowing stuff. They naturally understand 'delayed gratification', even if they don't exercise it with their spending habits. They are happier to wait for something than their daredevil (annoying) brother.

- They happily squirrel their money away and they know what they are saving for. They are prepared, always prepared, and usually like things 'just so'. They know what works and stick to that, quite comfortable in the familiar, even when they know that the norm will ultimately not give them what they need in the long run.

- They can worry and be indecisive. They don't always take well to spontaneous changes of plan; in fact, consistency gives them confidence. Sometimes they limit their own creativity, preferring to stick with the status quo, especially if it seems to be working.

Dreamers

'Whatever happens, happens . . . we will end up where we end up' is their motto.

Dreamers (also called no-planners) can be creative, easily adaptable and at times unconventional. They are simply not fussed about money. They tend to be content with their life, usually having less than most but being OK with this. They are happy to let their partner take care of their finances.

They usually love their job, and are not motivated by money—which is usually a good thing, because following your passion tends to be a sure way to lower your income-earning potential.

While they don't think about money, a no-planner can only continue with this attitude if someone else is managing things, otherwise it eventually catches up with them. When it comes to money they can be easy-going, but this quickly turns into being disorganised. They are not trying to ignore their money issues—

WHO'S AFRAID OF FINANCIAL FAILURE?

Research—and common sense—suggests that downward mobility is far more painful than upward mobility is pleasurable. In fact, in the 1970s psychologists Amos Tversky and Daniel Kahneman gave a name to this bias: 'loss aversion'.

Most people, it turns out, are not just highly risk-averse—they prefer a bird in the hand to even a very good chance of two in the bush. They are far more cautious when it comes to bad outcomes than when it comes to good outcomes of the same magnitude.

The search for economic security is, in large part, a reflection of a basic human desire for protection against losing what one already has. This is felt strongly by the safety seeker, but less so by the financial adventurer who abides by the motto 'you have to be in to win'. These differing risk-profiles can create conflict later in life if your partner can't relate to your approach to money or wealth creation.

they simply don't register on their radar. Their partner might consider this irresponsible, but this is not their intention.

Being a no-planner does not mean that you are a no-hoper. Dreamers can have financial dreams of grandeur, but no executable plan to get them there. They have a tendency to put their faith in the universe. If someone was to help a no-planner develop a plan, then they can buy into it, provided their 'free spirit' is not too clipped in the process.

Signs your kids may be a dreamer:

- They are happy to go with the flow and hate being controlled. They will push back if they feel they are being restricted too much, especially if it flows over into their relationships with other people, as no-planners pride themselves on their relationships.
- They don't tend to worry about the future, which is good in the sense that they don't get too anxious about things they can't control, but they don't worry about much beyond their immediate friendships.
- They are generous and will do anything for a friend. They are loyal and compassionate by nature—a good friend to have, although best you don't marry them as you will likely go nowhere fast. They can be a bit flaky at times. They can work hard, but not alone. They need people around them to bring the best out of them.

DELAYED GRATIFICATION

We are taught that those who can develop the skill of delayed gratification are more likely to make more money, report higher levels of happiness, and to be more satisfied with their family, jobs and lives. The same outputs are demonstrated by those who are self-motivated. Those who study delayed gratification and self-motivation believe they are skills that can be learned, refined and developed.

For instance, scientists have found that people can get better at self-motivation if they practise. The trick is to realise that we are in control—not that we are exercising self-control (a different concept entirely), but that we have a choice. When people believe they are in control, they tend to work harder and push themselves more. They are, on average, more confident and overcome setbacks faster.

COMBINING CASH FLOW AND STRATEGIC PERSONALITIES

Like salt and pepper, Batman and Robin, strawberries and cream, some things are made to go together. When it comes to money personalities, the same thing applies, although not in the combinations you might expect. A combined shopper/dreamer personality is common, but so too is the shopper who likes to play it safe. The problem for this poor thing is that their tendencies are competing, which means they have the urge to spend money (or at least not save easily), but then they feel bad about it!

The saver and the safety warden combination is also common. They can go without, but don't have an effective strategy to take them forward faster. My husband is a saver and a no-planner. I am a shopper and a daredevil. My daughter is showing saver and security tendencies (just like her grandmother). My son looks to take after me.

Remember, just because you might be programmed differently to your child doesn't mean that you are better and they are worse. You each have your own challenges, that usually come to light when you try to combine your personalities with those of your partner.

Your kids are going to face this as well. Your job as the parent is to equip them with what they need to get through the hard stuff.

The problem with school is you are taught to conform, to follow rules. I can understand why this is required, as the very concept of trying to organise a group of more than five children horrifies me. But the things that make you succeed at school don't usually make you good at life. If anything, the two can be mutually exclusive. School teaches you to do exams, life doesn't care whether you pass or fail. School is politically correct, life is not. School doesn't encourage winners or losers. Life doesn't care about losers but loves winners.

As parents, we need to be aware that the ability to delay gratification is critical. What we might not recognise is that genetically, some of us are pre-set to find it easier to delay gratification (savers) and some of us aren't (shoppers). Delaying gratification comes more naturally to some than others.

It's not to say that delayed gratification can't be learnt, because it can, although much media hype doesn't cover this. It is also not to say that if you are a shopper that you are impulsive in all areas of your life, but it can be an indicator of your future, especially if your strategic personality does not combat the weaknesses of your money personality.

The marshmallow test—understanding delayed gratification

Most of us are familiar with the marshmallow test. It began in the early 1960s at Stanford University's Bing Nursery School, where Walter Mischel and his graduate students gave children the choice between one reward (like a marshmallow, pretzel or mint) they could eat immediately, and a larger reward (two marshmallows), for which they would have to wait alone, for up to 20 minutes. The study famously showed that individual differences in the ability to delay gratification on this simple task correlated strongly with success in later life. The ability to endure longer wait-times as a child was linked years later to higher SAT scores, less substance abuse and parental reports of better social skills.

What is less discussed is that the test didn't start out as a test, but as a situation where the students were studying the kind of things that kids did naturally to make self-control easier or harder for themselves. As Mischel said in an interview with Jacoba Urist of *The Atlantic*, 'The studies weren't initially about delaying gratification but more around understanding what influences a child to reach his or her choice.' Over time the kids could develop skills to delay their gratification and became less likely to eat the marshmallow (or whatever reward was chosen).

However, further studies, especially at the University of Rochester, have called into question the marshmallow test and some of the conclusions drawn from it—which I must admit was a bit of a relief to me, because when I tested my children, my son ate his marshmallow and then his sister's!

The Rochester study mixes things up. It highlights that being able to delay gratification is influenced as much by the environment as the ability of the participant. Interestingly, children who experienced reliable interactions (where the researchers had demonstrated that they would follow through on what they were offering) immediately before the marshmallow task waited on average four times longer—12 versus three minutes—than children in similar but unreliable situations.

Lead author of the study Celeste Kidd, a doctoral candidate in brain and cognitive sciences, said the results 'definitely temper the popular perception that marshmallow-like tasks are very powerful diagnostics for self-control capacity'. She says being able to delay gratification in this study not only reflected each child's capacity for self-control, but also their belief about the practicality of waiting. That is, some kids chose not to delay because they weren't sure that there would be any gratification to justify it. Personally, I would call these kids street-smart and possessing a skill needed for the next generation to navigate the changing world. Their gut was telling them something, so they went with it.

The findings provide an important reminder about the complexity of human behaviour, and how people's actions are based not only on temperament but also environmental factors. The Rochester results are consistent with other research showing that children are sensitive to uncertainty in future rewards, and with population studies showing children with absent fathers prefer more immediate rewards over larger but delayed ones.

What is shared between these studies is an acceptance that delayed gratification, which is considered part of your EQ (emotional intelligence), is more likely to indicate success later in life than your IQ. When I spoke with family therapist Diane Levy, she was keen to reiterate that developmentally, EQ is more important than IQ for success in life, and delayed gratification is an identifiable characteristic of someone with mature emotional intelligence. It is less about whether you can wait to eat a marshmallow and more about 'whether you can tolerate ordinary frustration, not avoid it but tolerate it, and have self-restraint. That is what marks the emotional maturity in a person.' This is an area where as parents we are starting to let our kids down—especially when we helicopter-parent.

Don't get me wrong—I have clients who in their field of learning have exercised huge self-control and discipline, but when it comes to money they are incredibly irresponsible. Mischel discusses in a later book (*The Marshmallow Test:*

Mastering Self-Control) the situation where certain people can exercise willpower in most areas of their life but at some point they get 'willpower fatigue'. He references Bill Clinton and Tiger Woods as examples of this, along with many successful people who have an almighty fall from grace at some point in their life.

There are many reasons for this, but the point to focus on is that people need to *develop* financial self-control to ensure they have financial self-control. You can hope that conquering one area of your life will cross over to you being able to exercise restraint in others, but if we want to develop financial responsibility and the ability to exercise self-restraint with money, then we need to practise this skill as it relates to money. This applies to our kids, too.

Like anything in life, you are trying to teach them in a way that is not so harsh that you or they give up. It's that combination of making it hard enough, but not too hard. If we want our kids to have good financial management skills, they must have something to manage. The savings goals must feel fair to the child to get their buy-in.

Self-restraint in finance is probably more challenging for privileged children who could have everything. So as a parent who can afford to be generous, thought needs to be given to whether our generosity is going to feed into their genetic weaknesses or help them develop the skills they need to overcome them.

CONFIDENCE

The fourth and possibly most influential component in determining your relationship with money is how confident you are with it. One of things that builds financial confidence is being able to talk about money openly and honestly. A US survey by

T. Rowe Price on 'Parents, Kids & Money' found that financial confidence was based on whether kids and parents talked about money together: two-thirds of children whose parents frequently talked about the family's finances said they felt smart about money, while only 37 per cent of children whose parents *didn't* talk about finances felt the same.

Financial confidence also comes from knowing what you need to do and being prepared to do it at the right time, and from knowing when you need to get help—not just when you're sinking, but also when you want to be financially awesome. When it comes to getting help, not only do you need to be able to identify *when* you need it but also *who* you need to speak to.

Over time, as you learn what actions trigger certain financial outcomes, you build financial confidence, and self-assurance grows out of developing a plan for financial success and being able to achieve it. On the flipside, the fastest way to lose confidence is if you find yourself putting in effort but don't see any results. Too many people make the wrong financial decision and that then leads to an unwanted financial outcome, but they fail to understand the detail of what caused the problem in the first place. Instead, they usually form an inaccurate view of things and, with that view in mind, set about on a problematic course that they could have otherwise avoided.

Practice with money builds competence with money, and competence with money leads to confidence with money. For many of us, the safest time in our lives is when we are still living in the family home. This is therefore the perfect environment to start exposing your kids to the implications and realities of financial decisions. Confidence is a learned mindset, and it comes from exposure to financial realities, from demystifying the relationship between effort and reward, and from getting the results you expect when you expect them.

LAYERS TO MONEY DECISIONS

Every financial decision is underpinned by a set of precursors.

The outside layer, the one we tend to see, is the financial impact of an action or inaction, the financial detail of how the money being earned or spent fits into your overall money situation or financial plan. This layer is the quantifiable financial impact of a choice. We usually focus on this layer because it is visible.

The second, less visible, layer is the 'how and why' supporting those financial details. These are the reasons sitting underneath every financial choice. The reason is not always obvious, and it can stem from key assumptions made or the value you place on money.

To understand these assumptions, you need to look closer again at the third, almost invisible, layer: your relationship with money. Your money relationship is driven by your money personality and your early and current environment, as well as genetics.

As parents we will directly influence our child's relationship with money. As adults, if we are struggling to make the financial progress we should, the impact of this is not ring-fenced to ourselves: it passes to our kids, who are going to face much bigger obstacles than we can imagine.

A lot of people don't make the right calls because to

them money is mysterious. They feel that way because they don't 'look under the hood' at their financial choices.

Many people look at their finances and see no further than their current position, which could be based on a numerical assessment (I own this, and I owe that), or how they are feeling (in control, with a plan, or out of control). It is not always as easy as saying 'I want to do things differently', especially if their money personality or their relationship with money makes this challenging. However, if you can understand the reasons or choices that underpin your financial reality, you are better equipped to make the right decisions.

Using the analogy of layers, you could say that a well-lined jacket makes the jacket warmer, provides better shape, adds protection, smooths the finish and most importantly makes the jacket more durable. Your job as a parent is to provide your children with a financial 'life' jacket, one that is lined, durable and stretches as they grow. Your parents have directly influenced your own money personality and you will do the same to your children.

CHAPTER 4
CREATING THE FINANCIALLY INDEPENDENT CHILD

KIDS AND MONEY—WHEN DID IT START TO CHANGE?

The issues around kids and money are more complex and challenging than ever. Companies are aggressively targeting kids as consumers and have more tools to do it well. Parents have to compete for their children's respect and attention.

This change in the financial landscape started in the 1980s, when the term 'self-sufficiency' emerged as a value that equated to virtue and discipline. This new attitude started with trying to reform the welfare system, and pushed up into the everyday experience of the middle and working classes.

Self-sufficiency was possible because everyday people were

now getting access to financial information, stock markets and the tools needed to build wealth. Prior to this, access was restricted to the rich or privileged few. As with many great inroads of progress, the mantra of self-sufficiency, while virtuous, was also a way of pushing financial responsibility on to the individual. With this increase in responsibility came the opportunity to better your lot, and the 1980s gave many people the opportunity to change their financial landscape.

Following the 1980s came the internet and the notion of being your own 'free agent'. You could set the tone of the life you wanted to live. The possibilities were endless, or so it was positioned.

In the 1990s the stock market and financial information became accessible online and in real time. Financial literacy became a 'thing'. The economy was growing and with it the middle class were becoming wealthier, or at least had more money or credit at their disposal, which made them feel wealthier. It seemed that each generation was becoming wealthier than the last, because they had access to more money. Following on from this came an inclination to indulge children, which then facilitated a slower though still inevitable transition into independence.

Previously, we were encouraged to spend less than we earned, to buy a house and to keep working until we retired. That was all you had to do to ensure that you had a comfortable existence. Provided you hit these basic benchmarks, you could pretty much afford to coast along and everything would sort itself out.

But with progress came complication. Financial literacy widened beyond 'living within your means' to include the concept of good debt, bad debt and unproductive debt; credit, financial products and the ways you grow wealth. As this was happening, women were increasingly entering the workforce, divorce rates were rising, and many people were having to 'start again' financially, usually on the back foot.

For many years the government has kind of been our 'get out of jail free' card, ready to support us in our retirement years. But now we have started living longer, the number of baby boomers has started to impact on our ability to grow the economy, and we need immigrants with money to bolster it.

MONEY ISN'T EVERYTHING . . . UNTIL YOU DON'T HAVE ENOUGH

In the name of productivity, today's organisations are required to work smarter, which for some just means you fire a whole level of employees and make the remaining employees work harder or do more—which, in my view, although solving the problem short term, is not really a sustainable option. But let's not digress. Let's just say we are working harder than ever before, meaning we are tired and we want treats. In fact, we feel like we deserve treats. So we spend money we don't have on things we don't really need, but feel we deserve and are told we deserve now. We put off what we really want most (security for our family, an enjoyable retirement, to be mortgage-free) in exchange for having what we want now.

Money becomes emotional. In fact, it probably has always been emotional, although you are not forced to confront this until you don't have enough or you are not getting what you want despite trying hard. We are now taught that we deserve things, so we should have them, even if we can't afford them. Much of the economic pressure we are facing today is caused by mismatches between desires and the income of the family. The standard of living we enjoy is higher, but our level of satisfaction is lower. Credit levels are high, too.

Against this backdrop, our youth are emerging. High global unemployment, high misemployment or underemployment, unstable economies and restructuring industries are all around us. We are told disruption is a good thing, and maybe it is—unless it is your world that is being disrupted. With this disruption (buzz-word) comes opportunity (another buzz-word), and a whole lot of anxiety. So we need to ensure our kids have the most crucial of money skills:

- Cash flow management—spending less than you earn.
- Being able to save and invest.
- Understanding what life costs and therefore what you need to earn.
- Being able to start a business and run a business, as self-employment grows.
- Having a financial plan to bridge any income gaps.
- Understanding how to develop agility and adaptability.
- Understanding how valuable grit is, and how to develop it further.

If you as a parent haven't mastered these skills yourself, then you are going to have to master them quickly, or delegate the responsibility of teaching them to your kids to someone who has. But do not pretend everything will be OK if you do nothing. It won't be. You need to purposefully design a strategy to equip your kids with the tools they need to survive the financial landscape they are entering. And you giving up your own retirement to fund a child when they should be independent is no longer an option.

Do not expect your kids to listen to you, unless you are mastering these skills yourself. Just as some animals smell fear, a teenager sniffs out hypocrisy with the merest whiff.

Parents speak to me about these issues because they want their kids to avoid the money conflicts and anxieties they experienced and not have to deal with the mistakes they have made. Because of this ever-changing, constantly improving, moving-faster-than-ever-before world that we live in—that we have ironically helped to shape—it is imperative that our kids start to develop attuned money skills. They have to be better than us, because being average does not mean middle class, it means poor.

HOW EXPENSIVE IS PARENTING?

Pretty much every decision you make as a family involves money: whether you will earn it, or choose not to; whether you will spend it; if you can afford it and so on. Parenting is a thankless task. Parenting is an expensive task. How expensive might surprise you.

In a paper by Iris Claus, Geoff Leggett and Xin Wang, 'Costs of raising children', which was presented at the New Zealand Association of Economists' 2009 conference, the authors determined the average estimated expenditure by households with different incomes on a single child aged 12 years or under, and a child 13 to 18 years old. It makes for fairly depressing reading. The results, not surprisingly, show that parental expenditures increase as household incomes rise, with high-income households on average spending more than twice as much on their child as low-income households. Again unsurprisingly, the costs of teenagers were found to be higher than those of children 12 years or under. On average, low-, middle- and high-income households spent respectively 33, 20 and 12 per cent more on teenagers than on children aged 12 years old or under.

Average estimated weekly expenditure for raising a single child			
Level of income	Average weekly income	Age 0–12	Age 13–18
Low income	$704	$147	$196
Middle income	$1365	$243	$291
High income	$2838	$426	$477
Average income	$1552	$268	$316

Costs as a proportion of income

Although the estimated expenditure on raising a child rises with household income, the proportion of income spent on the child was found to decline. Low-income households spent about 21 per cent of their income on a child aged 12 years or under and 28 per cent on a teenager. This compared with, respectively, 15 and 17 per cent for a high-income household.

High-income households with a child had on average an income about four times higher than the low-income households, but spent less than three times as much as low-income households on a child 12 years or under, and less than two and a half times on a teenager. Also, the proportion of income spent on older children fell faster as income rose than the proportion of income spent on younger children (falling from 28 to 17 per cent compared with a fall from 21 to 15 per cent).

So the upshot is that these little critters cost a lot to raise, and the lower your income the greater proportion of it they take. The longer they take to leave home the more they will cost you. Unfortunately, the more they cost you does not relate to how likely they are to be financially successful—and in some instances it's quite the opposite. So let's start to dig a bit deeper.

Average estimated weekly expenditure for raising a single child as a proportion of household weekly income (in percentages)			
Level of income	Average weekly income	Age 0–12	Age 13–18
Low income	$704	21%	28%
Middle income	$1365	18%	21%
High income	$2838	15%	17%
Average income	$1552	17%	20%

HOW PARENTING HAS CHANGED

There is a general sense that parents are becoming more indulgent with each generation. Our version of what a childhood should look like changes with the passing of years, but it is universally agreed that indulgence leads to less well-honed habits, or the wrong habits forming. If money is too freely given, then concepts of delayed gratification are harder to instil.

The ability to delay gratification is a key life skill, along with self-motivation. If you don't have to wait to buy something then you become a sucker for credit, spending beyond your means and not tempering your expectations to your ability to earn. This has always been a challenge of parenting, trying to avoid creating an 'entitled child', but more so now.

Kids are usually unaware of how generous you are as parents. They remain disconnected from the financial realities of life until you introduce them to them. As we know, you never notice the tail wind behind you, if you have had it your whole life, until you don't have it anymore. But if our children say to themselves on a subconscious level, 'I want, I get', we are in part to blame as parents for facilitating that (by giving them what they want all the time). We are not necessarily creating a character flaw, but it is a problem that will create a weakness.

John Cowan of The Parenting Place says that 'One of the habits of successful living is to do the hard thing. If things come to you too easily, you don't have the gumption, spine, perspicacity to do the hard thing. As a parent you need to show your child that doing the hard thing creates a reward.' This is further supported by child and family therapist Diane Levy, who says of the trend of parents trying to be their child's friend: 'This is a choice, and at some moments in time you need to determine if you are willing to be a friend or a parent. If a parent is required, friend can wait until they are adults.'

SUCCESS, CHORES AND WORK

As a parent, we have the option of doing chores around the home ourselves, to delegate, or a bit of both. As we know, the problem with asking our kids to do something is that the chore becomes more of a chore than it needs to be. There are many times when I have thought it would be easier, faster and involve less conflict if I simply did the chores myself. What is interesting, though, is that a common feature of successful people is that they did chores as kids. Doing chores does pay off in terms of character, as it teaches kids that they 'can do what they wanna do, once they have done what they gotta do'. It teaches them that they can do boring and hard. It teaches them time management. And it teaches them to work for a reward (that said, not all chores should be paid for—more on this later).

There is a social shift in the next generation's attitude to work. For us, and our parents before us, work connects us to our status as a person. This view is shared less by young people, especially as many parents provide them with a comfortable lifestyle, usually at the expense or compromise of their own retirement. Kiwis are a bit useless like that. Our culture of apathy doesn't work when it comes to financial matters.

As a financial advisor, I see parents spending money they don't really have on buying their kids things they don't really need. As a parent I can relate, but as an advisor I can see a lack of recognition that this behaviour is going to make things much worse for our kids in the future. As a manager, I expect my team to provide me with all information—good, bad and conjecture—so that I can make informed decisions. We are wanting our kids to make informed decisions yet we withhold key components that enable them to do this.

Cowan, in assessing the effects of helicopter parenting—where we disconnect our kids from reality and swoop in to rescue them when things get tough—claims that 'Anything you do for your kids that they could do for themselves is robbing them of the opportunity to learn resilience and self-dependence. It does cut across our loving hearts, especially when it can be easier to do it yourself. But it is not a positive, as we are robbing them of their opportunity to develop resilience, self-esteem and confidence.'

Of course, parents want to be liked. Cowan speculates that maybe we are not as secure in our role as parents today. Parental authority is not a quality that is greatly espoused by anyone these days. Parents in earlier generations would not have needed 'permission' to do certain things for their kids.

We seem to have a more humble approach to parenting, which in general is nicer, but it can rob you of your authority. I am going to serve my kids by giving them the best childhood I can, but in doing this I still intend to instil in them a good work ethic and the ability to delay gratification.

Children not respecting their parents is always a challenge. A huge tool is for parents to model respect, for others and in your behaviour towards money. But first you have to have respect for yourself.

THE ENTITLED CHILD

A lot of the parents I have spoken to over the years fear that they will create an entitled child. As a parent, this has crossed my mind more than once.

The most effective way to combat a sense of entitlement is to teach your child to work. Show them the value of a dollar and how much work went into making the money. We have to encourage our kids to discover the dignity of work and earning money for themselves. And if they run out of money, be prepared to say no to giving them any more.

It takes both strength and resolve to say no to your kids, especially when you know you have the ability to give them exactly what they want. But you have to let your kids suffer the consequences of their decisions while they are in a safe environment in which to do so. If they have no money, tell them to get a job. Don't give them money, otherwise they will never get a job. Yep, there will be times when you cave, and you will bail out your kids because they make a dumb mistake, but if you rob them of the learning experience of cause and effect, you are setting your kids up to fail big. As a parent your job is to let them fail while they are under your control, where you can manage the outcome. Allow them to learn the lesson, but not so intensely that the spirit of the lesson is lost.

In our house, if all the family chores are done during the week, we go out to dinner as a family. The kids love it. I love it. My son, who is a little bit dapper, and also a bit of a poser, loves to dress smartly on these occasions. He wears a white shirt, tie and blazer. For him, family dinner out is the best night of the week. He gets to dress up and order the dinner and drink (excluding Coke or Fanta) of his choosing. And he gets dessert. Mum and Dad are happy because we have not had to cook dinner and there is usually a good vibe. I can see why they love it, because I love it too.

But for the kids to be allowed to come to the dinner, they need to have done their chores. These are chores that we don't link to pocket money. They are chores related to being part of a family and living in our household. Chores like making their beds, tidying their rooms, emptying the dishwasher, taking the washing basket to the laundry. Basic stuff that we all need to do, to share the load.

We have a system where the kids put a tick beside each chore on the days that they do them. They are allowed certain days off for some chores (for example, they don't need to make their beds on the weekend). However, their job is to complete a certain number of ticks each week to qualify for the family dinner.

One week, for a variety of reasons, Cameron didn't get the required number of ticks to qualify for dinner. I went into his room when I got home from work to find him getting dressed to go out. I told him that he didn't qualify for dinner and he wouldn't be going. Cameron then had a dramatic meltdown, telling me he didn't realise (I am not sure how this could have been the case, since we had gone over it several times and the rules are written on the whiteboard above the chore amounts). But that is Cameron, always pushing—a great trait in an entrepreneur, but an annoying trait for a parent to deal with. When he realised that I wasn't going to give in, he took to blaming the system (largely me) and how it wasn't his fault as I didn't make the rules clear and so on. And when that didn't work, he starting winding himself up. He was crying and I was starting to waver. But then I thought, sod it. This is what life is about and I need to prepare him for life. So he didn't go to dinner that night. In fact, none of the family went to dinner that night. I must say that one of the most unfair things about disciplining your child is that you often have to sit through the lesson with them and go without, alongside them. Not going to dinner that night worked as a good lesson for all of us.

You would be right in hoping that Cameron would have learned his lesson by this point. But as it turned out, he didn't learn the full lesson. Yes, he learned that if he didn't do his chores, Mum was serious about the consequence. But he also learned that if he didn't get the reward, then no one else got it either.

A few months later we had the same issue around Cameron not getting his ticks. In himself he was OK with not going to dinner, and he recognised that he didn't qualify for the perk of a family dinner. On one hand, this was a bit of a parenting win. But the thing that bugged me was he told his sister that she wasn't going to dinner that night either because he hadn't gotten his ticks (even though she had). She wasn't fussed one way or the other, but I sat them both down and told them both that Dad and I were going to family dinner and that Maddie could come if she wanted. Cameron would be getting dropped at his Granny's and not come to dinner because he didn't do what we agreed. Maddie was given the choice of going to Granny's or coming to dinner with Mum and Dad. She opted for dinner.

Cameron had a bigger meltdown. But I followed through.

He has not missed his ticks since.

I continue to have my authority as a parent challenged, and I continue to stick to my guns about chores being a necessity of family life and the fact that some chores don't come with a financial reward. Ending up with a spoiled or entitled child is a common fear for many parents. If you find that saying 'no' to your child is more of an emotional challenge than it is a financial necessity, then you must be more purposeful in setting financial limits and implications. The more financially generous you are with your child, the less likely it is that they will be financially resourceful or hard-working. Too much financial generosity risks giving your children a sluggish financial metabolism that will mean they're a little bit (or a lot) useless later in life.

THE WALL OF SILENCE

When I meet with my clients for the first time, I often ask them how they would describe their money personality and where they learned their money behaviour from. I ask what their parents taught them about money, if anything.

More often than not, your behaviour as a parent will be the strongest influencer of your child's financial behaviour for the first five to ten years after leaving home and, if you have been financially unsuccessful, longer. Most children's habits come from copying the behaviour of the people they interact with most closely, usually their parents. Most commonly, your kids will spend like you, save like you, give like you, budget like you and fight with their future spouse about money just like you.

Even though we intuitively understand this, for many families there is still a wall of silence between parents and kids when it comes to money. Many parents that I work with have incompatible money personalities, and sometimes disagree over their shared financial goals, but the one thing that unites most parents is the desire to have their children be better with money than they are.

However, when it comes to money, it is what your kids hear, see and feel at home that will impact upon them most greatly. Equally, what they *don't* see or hear can have just as great an impact. I am meeting too many families who don't set time aside each week to discuss their finances. I understand the reasons why: too busy, can't be bothered, I don't want to fight, or I just don't have the energy after working full time, going to kids' activities and tidying the house. All these points are valid, but all the kid takes from it is that money doesn't need to be discussed because it isn't important, or that it just sorts itself somehow. A passive or nonchalant approach to money can actually have more of a damaging effect on a child's understanding of money than you realise, because not only are they not developing the tools they need to navigate adulthood successfully, they are at a greater disadvantage still, because they don't even know that there are tools to be developed. Knowing what you don't know is one thing. Not knowing what you don't know is another thing entirely. They remain blissfully unaware and ignorant. And when it comes to money, ignorance is dangerous and leads to a delayed transition towards financial independence.

While the desire to help our kids is evident, and most parents agree that providing financial guidance for their kids is their responsibility, research shows that more than 65 per cent of parents have no idea how to actually do this. This figure is based on studies in America, where people tend to be more financially literate than us Kiwis, so I can only assume that in New Zealand fewer still have a plan of attack of how to help their kids. Further research has suggested that of the few families that are teaching their kids about money, parents are much more likely to discuss bigger issues around investing, how credit cards work and entrepreneurship with their sons than their daughters. Daughters are more likely to be taught about giving, rather than making money.

While I buy into the notion that the female is often the glue of the family, especially if they are a stay-at-home mum, young girls' sense of financial confidence and worth can be compromised by this. I see this play out with my older female clients, who are generous to a fault. Many find it easier to put themselves last, because that is what they have been taught to do. This simply doesn't work when you are single, when the buck stops with you. So many of the financial values women are taught are based on the assumption that we will meet the right person, who will treat us right, and we will be with them for the rest of our life. As we know, this is simply not the case for more than 50 per cent of adults, and the inadvertent lessons we programme into our girls do not adequately prepare them financially for living alone.

We now know, thanks largely to the fallout from the Global Financial Crisis (GFC), that good financial habits are not inherited, but instead perfected with instruction, coaching and practice. It would be easier if financial education could take a one-size-fits-all approach; but in reality, the nuances of each person's individual situation requires a tailored solution for each different person.

The young people I have spoken with claim their parents seem to find it easier to discuss sex and drugs than to have the money conversation. Parents need to get comfortable having the ongoing money talk. The earlier you start, the easier it will be.

The thing with money is that we already have some natural tendencies that are intertwined with our DNA, so the method of teaching or the emphasis you need to put on various aspects is different for different children. This makes things a little challenging, but the one thing that a parent knows is their children. Very early on, a parent probably knows their kid better than they know themselves. The task is to identify different tendencies early on, then to work on developing each child's skills to combat their weaknesses as well as enhance their strengths.

The objective is to create financially independent children. For most, this will not naturally happen. Instead, we have to build a process of learning to ensure that children are exposed to the right principles at the right times, to be 'forewarned and forearmed' for the stages at which they will need them.

Having said all this, I do not think that all money learning need to come from the parents. In fact, as kids get older I believe they need to hear some of the lessons from someone who is anyone *but* their parent. But the role of the parent is to ensure the conversations are being had by someone, whether it is a friend or family member, or if you have to pay someone to have them.

Remember, financial wellbeing is one of the cornerstones of general wellbeing. We want our kids to live good lives.

TEACHING OURSELVES AND OUR KIDS THAT IT'S OK TO FAIL

A lot of people make huge, expensive mistakes as adults simply because they were never allowed to make small, inexpensive mistakes when they were kids. Many parents try so hard to protect their children from the pain of a hard lesson that they never develop the mastery that comes from experiencing failure.

As a parent, you will probably take little joy from the process of letting your child make a mistake or fail. Usually I feel sick about it, and seek comfort from my husband or parents that I have done the right thing.

But like it or not, our children are going to learn some hard lessons in life, specifically when it comes to money. It is not a question of when they make a mistake, it is a question of how big the size of the mistake will be that will make them learn how to control their spending.

As a parent, your role is to help them learn when the stakes are low. Making a stupid buying decision when you are 12 isn't quite as devastating as making a stupid career choice and incurring a student loan for the privilege of realising you don't want to work in that field, or marrying a financial dud later in life.

STEPS TO SUCCESS

The desired output of our parenting journey is a financially independent child. The input is a whole lot of lessons, exposure and practice.

We start with a simple but solid foundation, then we systematically build, knowing that we are helping to create a child who can withstand the uncertainty of their time, and still pull ahead. Who will thrive. Who will be financially successful.

In an ideal world, you would start talking to your kids about money from as young as five. The lessons are pretty small when your children are younger, but when they hit 13, they need to be exposed to the realities of what life costs, as they are choosing subjects to study and careers to pursue. The shift in financial transparency is huge and conscious at this point. You are welcoming them to adulthood with a good bolster of real life. I have outlined the key stages below.

Each stage shows objectives of what the child needs to have

learned, and what you need to have spoken to them about. I have kept the age groups generic, but as a general rule it is important that at each birthday you are consciously passing more financial responsibility on to your child. You show them you respect them by giving them more and more financial responsibility.

Age	Theme/objectives
5–9	Introduced to the basic concept of money, where it comes from and how to consciously spend.
10–13	Building on the basics to more real-world application. Start to take financial responsibility.
14–16	Money means choice and with choice comes the need to plan.
17–18	Money is independence; real-world exposure and why failing can be good.
18–22	Time to leave the nest. What's my plan to fly?
23–30	How to be better, faster and smarter with money than your parents.

PART II
AGES AND STAGES

CHAPTER 5
5–9: THE BASICS OF MONEY AND HOW TO SPEND CONSCIOUSLY

Prepare the child for the path, not the path for the child.

This is the age when you start introducing the most basic of financial language to your children. By the time your child is nine, they need to know where money comes from, why we use banks to store our money and how to start to spend it. Most importantly, they must recognise that money is not magic*—it doesn't come from a never-ending supply and the 'hole in the wall' is not actually a special place that prints money.

Money needs to be introduced as something that can be seen and touched. This makes it real, and because it is real they can understand it better. Young children don't intuitively understand its value, but they do understand that more is more—so two

$1 coins will seem like more than a $2 coin, and three 50 cent pieces will also seem like more than a $2 coin. A $5 note may seem pretty much the same as a $20 note, although kids will pick up on the different colours of the notes.

Objectives:
- Teach them that you work to get money.
- Teach them that with money we must think about today, the future and other people.

Key conversations:
- Discuss that money is not magic.
- Discuss why we share, save and spend.
- Determine value-based chores.
- Start paying pocket money.
- Set up a money allocation system.
- Explain that we don't just save money, we also save clothes, jars, toys, books, etc.

Other developments:
- Illustrate what you earn and how it is spent.
- Give them a calculator as a present.

MONEY AND MAGIC

Although make-believe is an essential part of childhood, when it comes to money and magic, these two concepts cannot be room-mates. Your role as a parent is to help your kids comprehend quickly that money is earned. You do something to get it, and when you get it you have to spend it on certain things.

With the use of EFTPOS and credit cards we create a very

dangerous idea about money for our kids. Kids are too young at this age to really understand the concept of money, as they don't really understand the idea of cause and effect. To understand something they need to experience it, to see it or to touch it. From their perspective, when we use that swipe card it is pure magic, as it seems to let you do whatever you want, whenever you want. And when you need more, the hole in the wall gives it to you.

In wanting to create a childhood full of opportunity, we often can walk that fine line between opportunity and them becoming spoiled. When I feel that I have crossed over too far towards the dark side, I might say that we do not have the money to do something, to which my three-year-old rebuts, 'But Mum, just use that card.' I discuss how to get ahead of this argument below.

To help show kids the reality of money, it would be great if we were all paid cash in an envelope each week, then we brought that envelope home and divvied it up into envelopes for each of your planned outgoings. In a child's mind, this would create a clear connection between the parent going to work, receiving money for working hard, bringing that money home and allocating it before spending. That would be perfect. Perfect, but impractical and not a sustainable option, as most families wouldn't be able to withdraw the money to do the allocation, then deposit it again before the next bill payment comes out. So for many kids money remains conceptual, and holds this kind of magic.

While paying for everything in cash is a pain, it does have clear benefits for showing kids of this age how money is spent. What I have my clients do is withdraw their food money in cash. This is a helpful illustrator of what money is budgeted for groceries and what money is left. Kids can see that notes and coins are 'real', and it benefits them to see you working to a cash system consistently for at least one cost category.

THE CASHLESS SOCIETY

Moving to a cashless society will create even more challenges for the young. It's hard enough teaching our kids what they need to know to be financially savvy. It has become harder with the introduction of EFTPOS and credit cards, and it will get harder again as we move further towards a cashless society.

It is probable that we will move to a completely cashless society during our lifetime. Notes and coins will be replaced with a new e-currency or digital currency. Sweden's central bank, Sveriges Riksbank, has said it plans to investigate the viability of issuing a digital currency and looks likely to issue digital currency first.

Although it may appear simple at first glance to issue an e-currency, this is something entirely new for a central bank and there is no precedent to follow. The way younger generations understand money is likely to be altered, and they will possibly be disadvantaged as a result.

Pertinent questions remain about what impact virtual currency and its related technological structures would have on traditional banking. In an article on Sweden's proposed digital currency, financial journalist Jason Murdoch wrote that many large banks and financial institutions are creating proof-of-concept projects around financial technology. Recently, in the UK, the Bank of England said it was 'looking for new opportunities' in the fintech (financial technology) space.

In every instance, there appears to be an acceptance that technological advancement will inevitably shake up traditional forms of banking. Computers, smartphones and tablets are ubiquitous, and access to the internet is everywhere. As Murdoch writes, 'If the market can make use of the new technology to launch new and popular payment services, why shouldn't a bank be able to do the same?'

This makes for some exciting advances in the way we use money, but equally, it could cause problems for those not in control of their money. Studies have shown time and time again that less value is attributed to cashless transactions. In a study comparing cash spending to credit-card spending (which is the current version of cashless), people valued credit card purchases as equal to 50 cents in the dollar when compared to paying for the same item with cash. Or put another way, it feels half as expensive, or people are willing to spend twice as much for the same item when using a credit card.

Another study indicates that using a credit card versus cash causes you to spend 30 cents more in the dollar than using cash. All studies conclude that the less transparent forms of money like credit cards and 'tap and go' tend to be treated more like 'play money' than real cash, and are hence more easily spent (or parted with).

What hasn't been accurately tested is whether this extends to your own money, as opposed to credit. Does using an EFTPOS card mean that you spend more than using cash? Possibly, but you can put some controls in place so that this can be worked around. The biggest problem with using an EFTPOS or debit card is that if it is on an account in which there are funds allocated for various bills, you can't see as easily if you remain on track between pay-days.

We do know that paying with physical cash elicits greater psychological pain than other modes of payment. It is suggested that this is because when we don't have to hand over the cold, hard cash, the actual purchase is 'decoupled' from the pain of paying for it.

HOW DO WE GET MONEY?

Apart from debunking the myth that money is magic, another key conversation you need to have during this time is how we get money. 'We get money because Mum and Dad go to work.' If there is a concept you want to drill into your kids, it's that work gives you money and money gives you choice. For kids under the age of 10, choice is a concept they don't understand, so we simplify it further—money lets you do things that make you happy. It allows you to help others, enjoy treats and plan for the future.

You reiterate that when you work for someone they pay you money. As parents we can either get this money in cash (show them cash), or have it paid into the bank. If we pay it into the bank, then the bank is looking after it for us. If we ask the bank to give us our money, they have to. If the bank is not open, they let us retrieve it from the money machine, where we have to show the bank who we are before they give us our money. If we don't have any money in the bank, then the bank doesn't give us any. So it is up to Mum and Dad to ensure that we always have enough money in order to pay for things.

Take your kids to the bank to see you depositing money. Let them see you giving it to the bank, so they can understand that you can then get back what you have given to the bank for safekeeping.

Another exercise to do with your kids is to show them in real money or play money what you earn each week. As I said above, it is not practical to live this way, but just once bring the equivalent of your pay home in a big envelope and divvy it up, showing how it is spent on the family's living expenses— allocating some money to food, accommodation, basic living costs, etc. The objective of the exercise is to show why parents work and how that allows the family to enjoy things. Depending on the age of the child, you may choose to use the notes of the same value, say $10 or $20, as the child might not be able to decipher the different values attributed to the different notes. If you use same-value notes, then your kid will get a sense of volume by the quantity used for each category.

You can then tell them that Mum and Dad could put all their money into a big jar or piggy bank, but because they need to get access to it lots of times each day, it's easier to carry the money in their wallet or leave it in the bank, who protects it for them.

At our house we designed our own currency to help illustrate this. This also has other benefits when it comes to pocket money, which I discuss later in this chapter.

WHY DO WE NEED MONEY?

Take the time to discuss that money buys independence, opportunity and a lifestyle. In kid shorthand, money has the power to make us happier. For a five-year-old, they need to know that money can help make them happy because it helps them buy food, live in a house and do things they enjoy, for example.

Between the ages of five and nine is when you start speaking to your children about what you are trying to achieve as a family, why Mum and Dad go to work and what earning money allows you to do as a family. This is when you need to discuss what your family values are and how each person contributes to the family goals. It doesn't matter how much of it sinks in; the idea is we are preparing them for their next money milestone, and before we can do this they need to understand how money helps you and others.

This was especially necessary in my house when I asked my son to do something and his reply was 'You are the parent, and that is a parenting job.' This led me to calling a family conference to discuss what the role of a parent is, what the role of a child is, how we work together as a family and how this affects the wider community. My daughter cried through the whole ordeal—she was not sure why she had to sit through this conversation when it used up her allocated screen-time for the day!

EARNING MONEY

The first pillar of financial management is: 'You go to work to get paid money. With money you have choices.' Currently, most kids are taught that when you get money, whether through jobs or not, you can spend it, give it away and put some aside to spend when you want in the future. Some of these principles are built on with more purpose and with a twist later in this chapter. But to begin with, you need to earn money to spend it. For most five- or six-year-olds, the way you get money is to do chores.

It is important as a parent that you make a clear distinction between paid and unpaid chores. In making your kids work, it is equally important to delineate between jobs that need to be done because we are members of the family or same household (like making our bed, tidying our room, picking up our toys, clearing the table). You don't get paid for these jobs—that is called sharing the load. It is for doing the extra chores that they will receive payment.

Why we do chores

Explain that there are basic jobs that each family member needs to do. It will differ from household to household as to what constitutes unpaid versus paid chores.

In our household there are some basic chores that we expect our kids to do without reward: make their bed, tidy their room, take the washing basket to the laundry, put their clothes away. These are mundane tasks. In most instances as the parent I could do the job in a fraction of the time, to a better standard, without any nagging or headaches—but that is not the point.

Research has shown that some of the most successful people in the world cite doing chores as a consistent theme in their growing-up. Even if this wasn't the case, think of the poor future partner of your child if they have not developed any discipline to do the most basic of house management tasks! Explain that doing the family chores entitles them to privileges within the family (screen-time, family activities, family entertainment, etc.).

As parents we have to help our kids strive for competence. According to Stanford psychologist William Daman, in his book *Great Expectations*, kids 'avidly seek real responsibility and are gratified when adults give it to them'. As parents we have lowered our expectations of what our kids need to do around the house, and in doing so send the message we expect little of them, and that it's OK to live mostly for yourself. It is because of kids' desire to seek real responsibility that I encourage you to share with them the underbelly of your family finances, but before you can do this you must first introduce them to the concept of working for money through chores.

Family therapist Diane Levy sees chores as an extension of compliance. 'When you ask a child to do something, they do it. As well as getting that sort of ordinary compliance through chores, you get self-discipline, self-restraint and competence. Chores help you build competence in one area, but from there you understand how you can become competent in other areas.'

POCKET-MONEY BASICS

The concept of pocket money is the single most important tool you need to introduce to your children before the age of nine, closely followed by how to spend it (see chapter 6), to set the right tone for future spending habits. How your children handle the money will be indicative of their natural money personality.

The role of pocket money will differ depending on whether or not your household is privileged, where the children have everything they need. If you are in a household where people are struggling and there is no money to pay pocket money, then you need to be encouraging your child to think of ways they can earn money outside of the family, whether it is walking the neighbour's dog, doing errands for the wider family or selling toys on TradeMe. The most important thing is that if there is no money to pay pocket money, you need to make it clear to your kids why this is so, what you are going to do about it, and what you want them to do about it.

THE OPPOSITE OF SPOILED

I read of Japanese children as young as six who serve and clean up lunch for themselves and their fellow students each day. T.R. Reid, who wrote a book about the years that he lived in Japan with his wife, said it was cute to watch these young children don chef's whites and serve others. Except it wasn't playtime. The school wanted lunch served, and the children were expected to complete this task, so they did. In the Western world, adults are paid to serve and clean up after children. It is worth noting that in national surveys 75 per cent of Japanese children cite working hard as a top priority; 25 per cent of American kids do.

As a parent, getting children to do chores often involves nagging. With so many indoor chores—chores that are just as easy for us to do ourselves—many parents are less inclined to push their children to complete them. It is not because these parents feel they should serve their children—they don't. They believe in the family 'share the load' approach. It is just they get sick of nagging. Sure you can reduce screen-time, activities, dessert, treats—but these things don't always create the desired assistance. Many of the parents I interviewed say that they feel they are telling people what to do all day, or are being told what to do all day, and when they get home they just don't have the energy to fight. 'I may be a bad parent, but sometimes I just want to have a conversation with my kid and not tell them what they are doing wrong or haven't done. I just want to listen to what they have to say.'

Parenting, at times, feels like one giant battle, and you must pick your battles. Many of us don't always have the energy to tell our kids to set the table, nag them about clearing their plates, making their bed, doing their homework, so we tend to think it is going to be easier for us to either do these things ourselves or not bother at all, because the idea of nagging seems like a waste of energy. (Although nagging can't be all bad, because in a UK study of successful women in the workforce, it was found that most had nagging parents—so maybe it has some positive spin-offs?)

When the financial environment your kids grow up in is disconnected from reality, you disadvantage them for success later in life. Kids need to work, period. Kids need to do chores, and not all chores should come with a financial reward. Some of the most successful people in the world have cited nagging parents and having to do chores at home as things that both grounded them and focused them on success. A parent's influence does not necessarily guarantee the success of their child, but it will usually determine the likelihood of them being a financial failure later in life.

When do I start?

There is no right time to start, but as a guide I would say pocket money should be paid from the age of six or seven, or earlier if they start asking you to buy them things. As mentioned above, with pocket money comes a requirement to 'earn' that money, so they need to be old enough to hold up their end of the bargain, and for you as a parent to be confident that you are prepared to follow through with the implications of them not doing their chores.

How much should I pay?

Again, there is no right amount to pay, but I suggest they should be able to do chores up to the value of their age. Therefore the amount of payment should be roughly linked to their age. So, if a six-year-old was doing an hour or so of jobs per week (outside of her family, unpaid jobs), then she should expect to be able to earn $6.

Set up a job board

Write a list of age-appropriate jobs, outside of the basic family chores, each with a value attached to it (e.g. mow the lawns $10, clean the deck $1, bring the wood inside $1, empty the dishwasher 50 cents, chop the wood $5, etc). It should be that in doing roughly one to two hours' work over the course of the week they should be able to earn their age in pocket money. The monetary reward needs to be linked to the time involved for each task.

In our household the amount that can be earned each week is uncapped, because we are trying to teach our children that the harder you work, the more you get.

For kids that are naturally lazy, or don't see the need to earn money because you pretty much fund everything they want, this is your chance to explain that they can earn money to spend on other things that you are not going to pay for. Be clear as to what costs you are not prepared to pay for, so they have an idea of what the money they will earn could go towards. For example, I don't pay for them to buy apps on my phone. If they want them, they have to pay for them themselves, after asking for my permission. (I learned this the hard way and put this rule in place after my son downloaded $9000 of in-app purchases in the matter of one hour. Each purchase was $150, if you please!)

How do they get paid?

- Explain to your kids how you plan to pay for their work. In a way, you are their first employer.
- Take the payment seriously. Decide the payment day, and the frequency of payment. We pay weekly, every Saturday morning.
- Pay cash. It is important you pay cash or some currency that they can touch and feel. If they have a bank account, refrain from depositing the money directly into the account if the child is under 10. The lesson being learned is diluted if they cannot see and touch the reward of their efforts.
- Do not miss a pay-day. Make your payments dependable. Paying pocket money regularly is not just about paying your kids, it's about honouring your obligations. If you say you are going to do something related to money, then you have to follow through with it. This is hugely important groundwork for some juicier principles we will build on as they get older.
- Family therapist Diane Levy feels strongly that connecting the payment with something is relevant to your child's level of development. Levy believes that to say, 'You've done your chores, I've put the money in your account' means nothing. 'It means absolutely nothing to them. And if it's on a card, it means nothing going in and nothing going out, certainly for younger children. . . . But for all children I think what's important . . . is to honour the obligation. I don't think we should be casual about that.'

LEARNING TO SPEND—THE THREE-JAR APPROACH

One of the cornerstones to financial success is to be able to consciously choose whether or not to spend. The purpose of paying pocket money is to teach kids that when they earn money, they have more money to spend, which gives them more choices and a heightened sense of consciousness around their decisions.

The most popular way to teach kids about spending is to adopt a three-jar approach. Each pocket-money payment is divided into three jars, labelled spend, save and share. This creates some consciousness around how the money they earn can be earmarked for use now and in the future.

With each dollar they earn, you split the income into the different jars at a ratio you have set as the parent. If you don't want to use actual jars, there are many websites you can visit to acquire pimped-up and decorated containers to use for this three-jar approach.

Most parents set the ratio of the split at one third, one third, one third: so, for example, of every $6 earned, $2 would go in each jar. Other parents use different ratios. Personally, I prefer to put 10 per cent of the money into the 'share' jar, then split the difference 50/50 between 'save' and 'spend'. I like to set the 'share' jar at 10 per cent because this is the amount of my income I try to 'share' as an adult, and I want the principle to start early for my kids.

Because I want this to be a lifelong habit, I have started out getting them to set aside an amount they can sustain, should they choose to. But you do what you feel is best—there is no wrong split. How much you decide to allocate to each jar is at your discretion as the parent.

To prepare your child for adult life you should be encouraging

POCKET-MONEY FATIGUE

The problem with a lot of pocket-money arrangements is that the parents get payment fatigue—and the pocket-money payment stops or breaks down at some point. If this happens, in most instances it will undermine the whole purpose of the lesson.

A lot of the parents I work with complain of this happening, and of the general inconvenience of getting coins out of the bank each week. The system comes to a grinding halt because there will inevitably be a week or so where parents don't have the energy to withdraw the specific amount of money agreed, or they forget. Or 'the little sh*t doesn't deserve it'. For these reasons (because I could relate to all three common excuses), I designed and printed some money that allows me to pay my son's allowance at any point, because I have six months' worth of convenient and convertible money in my stash. On the back of the money is a note that says the money is redeemable for cash with 24 hours' notice, and the currency conversion ($1 for $1). I give his pocket money to him each week in a coloured envelope, with a list of the jobs he has completed attached, along with a tally of the money earned.

a lower spend percentage as they get older—as an adult, you are likely to have no more than 20–30 per cent of your 'spend' income left to spend on yourself, because it must first be used to cover your basic living costs—but for now the three-jar approach does what it needs to do.

The maths is simple and the lesson clear. It teaches kids that for any money you receive, you need to think about:
- tomorrow = 'save'
- today = 'spend', and
- others = 'share' or 'give'.

These principles never change over time.

While you might choose to tweak the rules to suit your household it seems to be universally agreed that:
- 'Save' is for your future self and is usually earmarked to buy an asset (not just toy junk).
- 'Spend' is for today and your enjoyment. Depending on the age of the child you can put rules on the spend category, i.e. they are not allowed to spend money on things which don't support your family's values. From their spending amount, they can spend money on themselves, presents for family or friends, and for those extra things they want that the parent is not prepared to pay for or things they lose that they need to replace (like the socks you keep leaving on the football field, Cameron). For example,

my son tends to be a bit wasteful. He loves hair gel but fails to abide by the recommended 'pea-size' drop, and instead uses a hunk of it each day. Instead of replacing this as part of our weekly shop, I make him spend his money replacing it if he runs out early. I don't care how much he spends on it (provided he can pay cash)—it's up to him if he wants to look around for a cheaper item or buy a smaller quantity of the item to save money. When he buys the gel, he has to line up at the supermarket, in front of or behind me, and pay for it in cash. What I am trying to do is show him the money he earns is not just for discretionary spending on fun and entertainment: it also has to cover his immediate wants and needs. For adults these would be better described as basic living costs, and when we cover these costs for our kids, they don't gain a concept of what that means.

- 'Share' is for charity—for others less fortunate than you or causes that you believe in. Personally, I encourage my children to give—not to give a specific amount per se, but to give. Have a discussion with your kids about how, as you earn money, it is good to think of others. That giving is a social responsibility but you give within your means. You give what you can, when you can. The idea of small but heartfelt giving is what we are aiming for when kids are under 10.

The problem with the jar system

The three-jar approach is a popular way of teaching money skills to kids between five and nine, especially when coupled with earning money. In fact, this approach appears in most books about kids and money.

However, while it is an appropriate tool for kids aged five to nine, when I looked further I could find no obvious evidence that the three-jar approach actually creates financially smarter kids. This approach has been used for many generations (my research suggests at least since the 1950s), yet the current generation is terrible with money. This forces me to conclude, on some level, that while not necessarily detracting from financial mastery, the jar approach in isolation is not providing the result we want.

I think the objective of the three-jar approach is sound. It is supposed to teach delayed gratification through saving, as well as being generous to others—two great concepts.

Problems arise, however, if you don't build on this base as the kids get older. In adult life, our kids will have little discretionary money left over after paying the bills, they won't be able to afford to give 30 per cent of their income away, and saving money to then spend it on themselves at a later point is still just encouraging them to spend.

I get the gist of what is trying to be achieved, and it is definitely age appropriate for younger kids, but it's not quite right for ages after nine. Research is showing resoundingly that we get better at spending (not saving) with each generation, and it could be because we are being taught to spend right from the word go.

Another reason why I think its effectiveness is low is that the approach gets tiring after a while, doesn't really relate to life, or can only be in place for a few years before it becomes outdated. It is too babyish for any child older than 10, and the approach to money needs to change as the child grows.

The basic idea of teaching kids to consider others and spend for today as well as plan in itself can't be faulted, but it is only the foundation. If you don't build on the foundation, all you have is a concrete slab.

The major concept that our kids need to learn from a young age is that you need to work to earn money. Money brings us opportunity and choice. Whether that choice is to allow you to enjoy more of today or save for the future is not the first lesson. The first lesson we learn is we must earn money.

MAKE SAVINGS GOALS VISIBLE

When we as adults set a goal, it helps our motivation if we are able to visualise the end result. The same applies to kids. If you or your child has decided to save for something, then help them visualise the end goal by getting them to cut out the picture of what they are saving for and putting it on the fridge. When I am feeling like Super Nanny, I then make a second copy and cut it into jigsaw pieces of different sizes, with each size roughly representing a value. The smaller the size, the smaller the monetary value attributed to it.

On the fridge we have a list of 'extra chores' and their attached values. The children have to determine which jobs earn which jigsaw pieces, and when they get all the pieces of the jigsaw, they get the toy or whatever else they wanted to save for.

WHY SHARE OR GIVE?

Some people will say that you must give in order to receive—which is true in most instances. But the giving we are encouraging in our young children is not so that they can receive something in return, but more so they can become aware of the wider community and its needs, as well as experiencing the joy of generosity. As they get older we need to teach them about successful giving, and how giving can work for and against you, if not done successfully. This point is especially relevant to our daughters, whose sense of self can revolve around pleasing others and giving of themselves. But for now, giving is about being conscious of others and being generous.

In the book *The Paradox of Generosity*, sociologists Christian Smith and Hilary Davidson present their findings of the 'science of generosity'. They look beyond those who give and why they give to the effect it has on the giver to be generous. Among some of the findings are lower depression rates experienced by those who donate more than 10 per cent of their incomes (41 per cent say they rarely or never experience depression, versus 32 per cent of everyone else.)

As part of your conversation with your kids, you need to make the connection that generosity does not only relate to money. It extends to giving of your time, your resources, your toys or your blood. Giving can include being emotionally available and hospitable—but for kids, the easiest teaching aid is the giving of money, clothes and toys. All these things will provide the psychological rewards of being generous.

The natural outputs of generosity include everything from developing a sense of self as generous, to being more socially networked, to being more physically active. Smith and Davidson argue that being generous involves neurochemical changes in the brain; more 'pleasure chemistry' is found in the brain-mapping of givers, providing a sense of reward for having done something good. Interestingly, studies have found that the more happy, healthy and directed you are, the more generous you are likely to be, although giving has to be practised consistently to offer rewards to the giver.

Much research has been done on the mindsets and psychology of people who give versus those who don't. People who give tend to have an attitude of gratitude and an abundance mindset. They buy into the ancient principle of whatever you give, you get back. You reap what you sow. They don't usually take a literal interpretation of this proverb in the sense that if I give $10, I will get $10 back in some form. Instead, they take the view 'If I do good, then I will receive good in some form, and even if I don't, I will certainly feel good.' I take the time to explain to my kids that giving shouldn't be laced with an expectation of receiving. Giving helps the recipient, but also enriches the life of the giver.

Many parents miss the opportunity to discuss giving with their kids—not because they are not giving, but because they are not being intentional about letting their kids see them give. The first time I told Cameron that we had been giving to a charity, he was shocked. With online banking, it's easy to do all your giving in two or three clicks. Much of the online experience robs you of the chance to make a powerful visual statement to your kids.

The giving 10 per cent rule stems from biblical teachings. In the biblical context, this money was to be used to support the widows and orphans of that time.

I personally love the idea of giving. I don't usually tithe to a church, but instead make the point of giving 10 per cent of my income to people who are less fortunate. At times I have not been as diligent as I would want—it's easy to spend that money on nothing if it's not directed to a purpose.

You choose a number that works for you. The idea of giving, at least in my mind, is about the spirit behind the gesture, not necessarily the amount itself.

I encourage my children to give, but I don't focus on a specific amount. It feels too contrived and against the spirit of the giving in the first place. I explain that, much like praying, it is a quiet thing to do. If they are going to do it, then no one needs to know they are doing it. They do it because they can and because it comes from the heart.

Sharing is an important part of any community, and there are many organisations that rely on the generosity of individual people, businesses and the government to function. Giving away some of your income can be a scary idea, especially if it feels like your income is scarce. One exercise you may consider doing with your kids is listing all the charities in your community. Discuss how, when little amounts come together, they can grow to be big enough to make a difference in one, or many, lives.

If your family does not have much money to spare, then other giving options include donating your time—perhaps helping with a local community project, or spending 30 minutes each month picking up litter at the local park or walking your neighbour's dog. Encourage your children to give their unwanted clothes or toys to families who have less than you. There are numerous opportunities to give of yourself, and you need to teach your kids how to do this. Let them experience the feeling of joy from being generous.

If your kids do give money to an organisation and it is a registered charity, then tell them to keep the receipt so they can claim it back on their taxes and get a refund. The refund is uncapped (up to the amount of income earned). If you claim back the donation and get a tax refund, you can re-gift the refund or keep it yourself, to offset against the giving and make it more 'affordable'.

A word of caution: females tend to be better at giving. It is part of their fabric and can be an approval-seeking behaviour that can work against them later in life. A child who shows a constant need for approval and who discerns that giving things away (toys, kisses, pictures) is a sure route to being liked may be giving clues you will need to keep an eye on as they grow up. As a parent, you never want to discourage the generosity of a giving heart, but sometimes there can be a fine line between a genuine desire to give and approval-seeking behaviour. Being generous in spirit and giving of ourselves is an attractive quality, but not if it is at the expense of your own financial health or financial wellness.

My kids and giving

Before we had kids, I was less concerned with who we gave to, and more interested in making sure that I was able to give. Now we have kids, we choose people and charities to support who are relatable to our family.

One family we support has an 11-year-old who is uber-talented at sport. He is a nice kid, a humble kid with a great mum. The dad no longer lives with them, which has put more financial pressure on the mum, and brought the matter to the fore as to whether he can afford to continue playing this sport.

As a rule, I am quick to point out that most of us don't get to do our hobby as part of our job, and that parents shouldn't fan the flame of doing something just because their kid is passionate about it. (I discuss this point separately below.) However, when it came to this kid, I felt that we were in a position to help the family and that this would be a great way of demonstrating the power of giving to my children.

I took the time to explain what we wanted to do to help this family, how we wanted to provide financial support. We had the family around to our home so that my kids could get to know them first hand. We talked about what this boy was trying to achieve and how we were helping him. He discussed what his goals were with Cameron, and what he needed to do to achieve those goals.

Separately, I am also coaching this boy on how he can use his talent as an opportunity for financial gain—transitioning him from being a kid who is good at something to a kid who has a real sense of being able to do what he loves and is good at, and leverage off this to make money. Those are two very different things.

My parents always gave 10 per cent of their income to the less fortunate. They tended to do this in the form of tithing or giving to their local church. My dad also tried to give at least 10 per cent of his time to help others. They gave even when I knew the situation was tight at home.

They never once told me that I had to give. They just said to me that 'to whom much is given, much is expected', and that they could afford to be generous, so they were.

Likewise, we encourage our kids to put aside 10 per cent of their earnings into the 'share' jar, but I do not make them. They choose to spend on what they want, and if they give more or less of it away, then that is their choice.

When parents' words and actions come together, it forms a powerful statement about the family's value system. I recall one time I had taken my kids to the bakery for lunch and we were walking back to the car. There was a homeless man sitting on the corner. My kids had never seen a homeless person before. They walked past him and kept staring. I don't think they were judging, but they were shocked.

Instead of me whispering 'stop staring', I decided this was a learning lesson for us all. I told the kids to huddle around and explained that the man we had just walked past did not have a home. He didn't have much food and he was hungry. I told them I would like them to go and give him what we had just purchased for our own lunch. We were going to do this because he needed our help and we were in a position to help him. The kids were shocked at what I was suggesting: firstly, about speaking with the man; secondly about giving him their food; and thirdly about giving him all of their food so they had none.

I walked back with the kids, stood by the man and asked Cameron and Maddie to pass him their food. He looked at me with surprise and at my kids with kindness. We said that we hoped he had a nice day.

I then grabbed each of my children by the hand and walked them back to our car. I didn't go back to the bakery—not because I couldn't, but because I could. The lesson that was being taught was that sometimes you give of what you have. Sometimes that means you don't have something for yourself. But it feels good to help people less fortunate.

The kids talked about that man all the way home. I explained that he didn't choose to have no home or job. Life had thrown him a curve ball and for whatever reason he was unable to catch it and run with it. We ate peanut-butter sandwiches when we got home.

CONCLUSION

The concept of pocket money is the single most important tool you need to have introduced your kids to before they are nine. We will systematically build on this concept but with more mature principles as we consciously create financially confident kids.

Pocket money isn't really about teaching your kids to spend or save. It's about teaching them that money gives you choices, and you need to earn money—it doesn't just magically appear. Earning money should translate to you having more money to do the things you want, after you have done the things you need to do.

One of the cornerstones to financial success is to be able to spend consciously. The purpose of the splitting of your kids' pocket money into spend, save and share is to bring some consciousness around money earned being earmarked for the future and now.

Giving is a worthwhile trait that doesn't always come naturally to all people. Teaching your child to allocate a portion of their income to 'giving' is an effective way of teaching them about sharing and that some organisations require the support of the wider community in order to function. Creating this consciousness breeds a more considered child, but remember not to place giving at the top of their list of financial responsibilities. Earning money is the most important task. How you spend it, including how much you give, comes after that.

CHAPTER 6
10–13: REAL-WORLD APPLICATION

Between the ages of 10 and 13 are the years to get kids confident in their knowledge of where money comes from and what you need to think about when you are spending (now, on others and in the future). The tween years are the last chance you will have to influence your kids' behaviour around money without your own behaviour being called into question!

This stage is about goal setting and introducing the concept of the family budget. Each year, new concepts are learned, practised and mastered. You are positioning and preparing your kids for future financial responsibility, so they can gain confidence and mastery around money. From the age of 10 upwards, it's time to step things up.

As discussed earlier, money represents the power and freedom to purchase or give as you see fit. In this vein, start discussing the difference between wants and needs with your children, as well as working with them to set goals which will help in overcoming the desire for 'instant gratification'.

Of course, some kids will find it easier to wait for something than others. This may be a sign of their money personality (shopper versus saver—see chapter 3) or simply an indication of how badly they want something. If your child is a saver or happy to 'live small', then they may have no need to spend. In this case, let them save more and don't encourage them to spend for the sake of spending.

Work with your children to establish an ongoing system of thinking about the future and putting money aside. Help them to determine how much to save, setting short- and long-term goals, then discuss where the balance should be spent and shared. Link saving with earning more and spending less in other areas.

Certainly, being able to walk into a shop and have your child spend their own money that they have earned on something they want is a powerful way to reinforce the 'work to earn money to get what you want' connection. It is quite exciting to see how your child has set a goal and managed to scrape together enough money to enjoy their purchase.

My first big purchase was a pair of Reebok shoes, my husband's a Walkman, and I am sure you can remember yours as well. It is a moment you don't forget, especially if you earned the money that facilitated the purchase, or went without to grow your savings faster. It is a moment to be remembered.

While I am not wanting to rain on anyone's parade, however, if we stop and celebrate for too long we could indirectly send our kids off on another tangent. As adults, we may have 10–20 per cent of the money we earn available for discretionary purchases. The rest of the money we earn goes towards making the turntable keep turning.

Kids need to understand the proportion of money that is available to spend on the here and now when they are adults, because it is seldom as high as 50 per cent of what you earn. Adjust their reality very early on, otherwise their perception of what life is going to be like when they are working will be distorted and can be hard to adjust to. If a child fails to transition quickly to the financial realities of life, then it will often translate to them getting into debt sooner, putting them on the back foot prematurely and unfairly. To some degree the parent will have contributed to this.

From the age of 10 you are preparing your child for the idea that adult life starts after they leave home. You have to start explaining to your child that your job as the parent is to teach them and equip them with what they need so they can be financially independent. You must take the time to purposefully build on the concept of saving and how it is for their future or for an asset.

Objectives:
- Determine their money personality and, with this, their opportunities and weaknesses (see chapter 3).
- Start setting savings goals and introduce the concept of planning.
- Start a living allowance and introducing life costs.
- Teach them the concept of compound interest as it relates to investing.
- Expose them to the entrepreneurial spirit.

Key conversations:
- Graduating your kids to the next level of financial education and management.

- Talk about why we earn money and why we think of the future.

Other developments:
- It is now compulsory for pocket money to be earned.
- A bank account needs to be set up. The savings portion of the pocket money should be deposited directly into the bank account; the spending element is to be kept in cash.
- For kids aged 13, a second account should be opened, for spending, with an EFTPOS card.
- Parents need to determine if they are on track to sort their own financial future, as no argument is stronger than 'Well you don't do it, so why should I?'
- Assign a grocery item for them to buy (whether it's something they use themselves or something that contributes to the family pantry).

POCKET MONEY IS NO LONGER OPTIONAL

From the age of 10, earning pocket money is no longer optional. Being involved in family chores was always compulsory, but earning pocket money through doing chores was not. If your child didn't earn any pocket money, then they didn't have money to spend or save.

For some kids, who didn't need or want much, not having money would not have been too much of an issue, because they could make do with what they had, or their parents' generosity supplied everything they wanted. For these kids, this next phase has a subtle shift of focus: that, as you get older, work is a requirement and no longer optional. If pocket money is not earned, then privileges are revoked. Screen-time, TV-watching, playing with other kids or sports—these things are all at your disposal to revoke as needed.

A 10-year-old needs to do $10 worth of chores, which should translate to one to two hours of work per week outside of the basic family chores.

SAVING AND GOAL SETTING

Learning how and why to save money is one of the most fundamental financial disciplines there is. Yet in my day job, I see smart people, who earn good money, still struggle to save.

If you want to set your child up for ongoing success, then you must teach them this skill, especially if it doesn't come naturally to them. It's not easy, and it certainly isn't always fun. But knowing how to save, delay gratification, set goals and priorities, make expensive purchases with cash instead of debt, cover emergencies and prepare for long-term investing is critical for any young adult leaving home for the first time and, probably more realistically, getting them ready so they can leave home. Kids should be starting to develop the knack of seeing something they want and working towards buying it from as early as six, although some start as late as 12.

If you do not have financial goals, you will be used by those who do. Yet too many people have neither a financial goal nor a plan. Apparently only 10 per cent of Kiwis over 50 have a retirement plan. If they end up where they need to be then it will be more a case of good luck than good management.

Talent alone has never ensured success. In fact, as former US president Calvin Coolidge once said, 'Nothing in this world can take the place of persistence. Talent will not; nothing is more common than unsuccessful men with talent. Genius will not; unrewarded genius is almost a proverb . . . Persistence and determination alone are omnipotent.' But if you are going to be determined and persistent, you need to know that you have the confidence, skills and tools to bring your goal to fruition. By helping your kids learn the language of money and business, as well as giving them financial confidence, you are giving them the skills to be able to live the life they want.

All financial goals need a plan: how much do you need (end game), what do you have (starting point), and how do you join the dots. When you set a goal, you need to accompany it with a decision to do more.

New choices = new actions = new results.

Family goals

The best place a kid will learn to set goals is from watching their parents do the same. I would encourage the family to sit down and discuss the things they want to achieve individually or as a family. Not all goals have a direct financial implication, but they will have a direct input that creates the successful output. Your role is to together identify the input to achieve the goal.

Common goals include going on a family holiday, going out for a special dinner, a parent getting home earlier, or spending more time as a family. The list can be as long and as detailed as you want it to be, although you need to select only one or two things that you are going to be working towards as a family. You need to detail the result you are after and what needs to happen to make it work.

It is best if all family members can contribute to the success of the goal. Give yourself a timeframe and check in every week to see how you are going. Create a family vision board and individual boards. Keep the family vision board on the fridge or in the most common area of the house, so that it is seen by everyone, every day. Measure progress against it. Celebrate the wins. If you want your kids to go after their goals, you need to show them that they are achievable and practise achieving them together.

Usually financial values vary between family members, especially if one parent is a shopper and the other a saver. A shared dream helps harness family energy and excitement in the growth of family wealth. There is no doubt that achieving financial goals is a lot easier when kids and parents are aligned.

If you have a family goal, then you all need to contribute to it. From the age of 10 onwards you need to be encouraging your kids to contribute. Write down the cost and work out how much needs to be saved each week for the goal to be achieved. For example, if it is important for the family to go on a family holiday, then each person needs to contribute 5 per cent of their income to the holiday fund, from the top earner to the children.

For young children, it is inappropriate to ask them to pay for their lodging! But if as a family you are all wanting to spend more on something than what you might usually (like a family holiday), then you all need to pitch in. To get buy-in from the kids, encourage them to research the holiday, make a budget and work out the cost. Then the kids can label the 'holiday jar' with different pictures that represent their goal destination.

For example, for one family holiday that cost $5000, my eight-year-old contributed $30 and my three-year-old daughter $3.50. At this age it's the gesture that counts, not the amount. It creates a sense of 'we are all in this together' and we all contribute relative to our own individual ability. This feeds into what 'sharing' means. Paying your own way, but paying for others when they can't afford to pay for it themselves . . . which is why the parents pay a greater portion.

Visualisation

Visualisation is a key trait described in the marshmallow test (see chapter 3) used by some kids to delay eating the treat. Many successful people are great at visualising the end game. For those of us who need to exercise the mental muscle of visualisation, an actual picture can be effective. It reminds the kids what they are saving for.

When I have felt slightly more creative, I have stuck the picture on to a piece of cardboard, then cut it up into jigsaw pieces, with each piece depending on its size having a dollar allocation, up to the purchase price. This then coincides with the list of jobs that sits on the board in the kitchen, each job with a dollar value. Your child then chooses which jobs he wants to do. As they earn the money, they put the puzzle together. When they have enough we go to the shop to buy the item.

The idea is to keep it interesting and engaging. The younger the child, the more visual the exercise needs to be.

Build excitement by tracking progress

If you are not making progress towards your own financial goals, then you need to change the way you are doing things, get help or see a coach. But do not let your kids see you attempt, fail and do the same thing all over again. That would be tantamount to financial suicide. If you want your kids to take their financial wellbeing seriously, then you need to too, as the parent.

In the absence of a clear goal and strategy, the results will be . . . not much. Unsurprisingly, the more certain the plan and framework a person is required to work within, the more willing they are to try to succeed—and they often will try harder than they even thought they could. If you want a person, in any situation in life, to give their best or to do better, then the effort and reward need to be closely linked. Kids are no different, but they can have a harder time breaking down the steps that lead them to what they want or where they want to be. Help them achieve their financial goals by working with them to set smaller goals, and by introducing perks or rewards where you can to keep them on track. But be careful not to rob them of their sense of achievement because you have made it too easy for them. One of life's sweetest treats is the taste of success born from your own efforts.

Saving success

One of the most satisfying things a child can experience when it comes to money is being able to save for something they want. There is an enormous sense of accomplishment for a child when they walk into a shop to buy something with money they have amassed. They have achieved something. Cheer them on. Visit the store as soon as possible after they have reached their goal.

For bigger purchases (like an iPad or GoPro, for example), to help keep momentum going, consider matching your child's saving contribution. Help them find jobs outside of the home that they could do, toys they could sell on TradeMe, or if they want presents for birthdays replaced with cash. If you do decide to match your child's savings, then you might want to put a cap on it, or contribute maybe 25 cents for every dollar they save.

Note: Just because you are creating teachable money moments does not mean you resign your role as a parent. You are still in charge and you can veto the purchase if you deem it unsafe or inappropriate.

It's always a fine line with parenting. Too many rules will become legalistic and too much grace becomes an enabling experiment. There will be some times when you need to let them learn that you can't or you won't help them out, and other times when you might be prepared to chip in if they have put in a sufficient level of effort themselves. You are creating a culture of success within the home environment—so create the right culture.

Priorities

There are times when you will need to tell your kids that you can't afford something, because this is one of life's constraints in the real world. However, sometimes the issue is not with the cost, but more in understanding what other costs or priorities could be changed to make something more affordable.

You are always in control of where the money goes and what it should be spent on first. When I am working with my adult clients, if they obviously can't afford something then I will tell them, but in many instances I instead try to determine how they could afford it. Together we think of options and scenarios, brainstorming and weighing up the implications of the options to determine if it is worth the effort.

With our kids, we want them to think outside of the box. To consider the opportunity of every decision. If I do this, then that means I can't do that. Or if I want to do this, then I must do that. Could they earn more, could they spend less somewhere else, what else could be done? What I have found is that people are prepared to do things they might not have otherwise been prepared to do if it allows them to have something they consider valuable or important. You just have to be able to brainstorm.

STEPPING IT UP—CONNECTING THEM TO THE REAL WORLD

Between the ages of 10 and 12, you are providing more financial opportunity and responsibility. We are wanting to introduce an allowance from age 13, but we need to condition our kids for this.

It may sound silly, but one of the tasks I had one family do was to give their tween $10 per month (not connected to her pocket money), to cover a specified household item. In this case, her job was to buy the family's toothpaste. She would canvas the family for their preferences and was encouraged to look for a discount and weigh up the value proposition of each item before deciding which brand she wanted to select. If the cost came in under $10, then she split the difference with her parents.

It's a simple exercise but oddly effective. You are introducing them to the concept of working to a budget or an allowance and the most basic of spending plans, and you are doing it in a controlled setting.

As they get older you can add more household items that they need to buy and provide an increased allowance to cover them. But at this stage, all you are trying to teach is that not all discretionary money is to be wasted; some of it is already pre-allocated to needs and they are in control of how much money is spent on what.

Another exercise to start conditioning them to manage their money is to give your child a budget for a family dinner. Give them the money allocated and tell them to ensure the meal costs less than the money given. Get them to take a calculator, just in case. Keep the receipts and do it again the next quarter. Whatever is left over, put in a jar (I love my jars!) and use it for another bonus family dinner.

Alternatively, instead of going out for dinner, have your child create a menu working to the allowance given. If they come in under budget, put the money in the jar and put it towards a bonus dinner in the future (or that night, if the dinner chosen needs improvement!).

ALLOWANCE TIME

From the age of 13, you need your kids to be making the connection between financial responsibility and personal independence. Up ahead are the years when your teenager starts going places with friends without parental supervision, stays home alone and starts making decisions for themselves. They start experimenting.

Too often this is the time when the conversation between parents and child becomes fractious. John Cowan from The Parenting Place offers some great tips.

- When you say no to your child's want, coach them to talk about 'what would help'.
- Sometimes by thinking out loud you can find creative ways to answer the problem, which is very much what the real world is like.
- Collaboration in search of a solution is the foundation of effective problem-solving.

At the start of each calendar year, when you set the annual family budget, discuss with your teen what is allocated to them for the year. Show them what this money has to cover. For example: we have allocated $5000 specifically to you this year. This is to cover your schooling, after-school care, football and dance class. In addition to this we have allowed $500 for clothes and half your mobile phone bill, and $200 for special events and outings that do not include the family.

Explain the costs that are non-negotiable (school and some activities) and what is at their discretion. Too often an unplanned opportunity or curve ball can crop up that somehow needs to be factored in. This happens to adults all the time. Whether you can afford the unplanned cost is less of an issue than you reviewing the opportunity in light of the plan already made. Look at what costs can easily be reallocated, what costs could be delayed, or what extra income needs to be earned to try to make the adjusted budget still balance.

This is the age when you start to give your kids an allowance to cover their clothes, entertainment and mobile phone use. Note, this is not pocket money, but an allowance.

An allowance is not an entitlement. It is a tool for teaching children how to manage money. Having a regular amount of their own income is the only way kids can learn to manage money. Real money gives children the ability to practise the pillars of money management, become resourceful and prioritise.

An allowance is their 'learning money'. They need to be able to make mistakes when the cost is minimal. If they use their own money they will think about how much things cost, eventually making smarter spending choices, and have a greater appreciation of things they have had to buy themselves. Remember, the purpose of the allowance is to give your children the opportunity to learn how to manage their money in a safe environment, where the cost of failure is small and you can still provide input.

One of the biggest misconceptions about an allowance is that some parents cannot afford to give their children 'extra' money. However, if you look at an allowance from a different angle, every parent can afford it. An 'allowance' is basically money that you are going to spend on your child anyway, just given in a different form. Instead of paying for things at the time your children want them, you pay them an allowance in advance and let them decide how to spend the money. The ultimate goal of an allowance is to teach children to distinguish between needs and wants and to prioritise and save—a difficult lesson that will be needed throughout life.

Obviously, you will need to set rules within some categories. For example, if you were going to set a $500 clothes allowance, your kids need to make sure they buy socks as well as a good shirt and jeans. If you don't trust your child to buy what is required, instead hold back a portion of the allowance to cover their most basic needs and give them the rest to spend. Initially, the list of what the money is to cover may be small, until they demonstrate an ability to spend within the constraints of the allowance.

You don't need to go full-throttle straight away; maybe give half the allowance one year, excluding some of the basics, and the full allowance the following year. It's about helping them build confidence, and making it clear what the allowance is expected to cover.

Make a list of what they are expected to pay for with their allowance. This solves the conflicts that may come up in stores. As their needs change, so can the amount—review it every six months.

It is critical that you sit down with them first and tell them exactly what they are expected to pay for from their allowance. Avoid paying their costs on their behalf, as it shelters them from reality. For example, if they need money to cover transport and phone, transfer this money into their bank account and have them budget accordingly.

Different children, different tastes

Different children have different tastes. Some have refined tastes for things like clothes, others don't care as much. When setting their allowance, set them up with a reasonable budget. I tell clients to use clothing chains Hallensteins and Glassons as a guide to what things cost when trying to determine an allowance. If these chains are too expensive, then use a cheaper reference, but just make sure the allowance is sufficient to cover what you would have spent on your child anyway.

ALLOWANCE TIPS

- If they don't earn money from their assigned chores, then privileges are to be revoked, but never the allowance. The allowance stands apart from pocket money, as money you would have spent on them anyway, but that they are controlling.
- If you have not done so already, you need to set them up a transactional bank account with EFTPOS or debit-card access. This account is different to their savings account, which was probably set up years earlier. By age 13, kids should have two bank accounts: one for savings and one for spending.
- Pay the allowance monthly. Stipulate what needs to be covered or purchased with the funds over that period.
- Have your child present their spending to you every quarter. Sit down and discuss what went well and the areas where they have struggled to make the allowance work. Discuss what they might repeat or do differently the next quarter. Reflecting on where you have spent the money is just as important as what was spent.
- Once you have given them their allowance, agree on the next check-in time, give them the option of asking you any questions during the next quarter, then walk away and leave them to make their own mistakes!

'I paid for it'

When you have your child pay for something out of their allowance, make sure you don't fall into the 'I paid for it' trap. Family therapist Diane Levy explains that when you make a child pay for something from their own money, it's theirs—you don't have control over it. So be careful what you let them pay for, in case you have need to confiscate it and get told 'but I paid for it!'

When it comes to cell phones in particular this can be an issue. If you tell your child to buy something for themselves, you need to consider 'whose will it be?'

Altering the allowance over time

As your kids get older, their allowance should increase to prepare them for independence. Start to include some bigger-ticket items: more of their clothing (maybe start with only one category, such as shoes or accessories), hobbies, entertainment, mobile plans and holiday spending.

While you can be sure they will make a few mistakes, they'll also learn from them. And it's better to make small mistakes now than larger ones later. By the time they are 18 they need to have a confidence around money that can only come from using and being comfortable with budgeting and the idea of money running out, stopping spending, and everything still being OK.

Reviewing spending

Show your kids that you open and review your bills and statements as they come in, as one of the principles of building a healthy relationship with money. Encourage them to take time each week or month to sit down and go through their spending against their plan, by showing them you do the same. This way, nothing gets lost, nothing gets overlooked, and there are no surprises the day before your payments are due. You are on top of it, and your kids see that you are.

THINKING ABOUT THE FUTURE

Becoming a teenager is a rite of passage towards adulthood. It's a big deal and with it needs to come a shifting of responsibility within the family.

This is the time to speak with your kids about what they want to be when they leave school, and connecting this huge step towards the workforce with real-life implications.

When I was seven, if you had asked me what I wanted to do, I would have said I wanted to be the manager of a fish and chip shop. When I was 13, my mum had me read the job section of *The New Zealand Herald* every weekend to get an idea of what jobs paid what. I had to do this for a year. My mum said I had expensive tastes, so I needed to be sure to earn enough money! She also observed that I liked responsibility and being in charge, with a tendency to march to the beat of my own drum, so I needed to consider if I wanted to be the boss or work for other people.

I then read, by chance, that 80 per cent of CEOs originally trained as an accountant. So I thought that was a safe bet. I did the necessary school papers, and never told a soul that I was going to train to be an accountant (that would be social suicide). But I knew it was a good grounding at the very least. So off to university I went, graduated, then worked at KPMG for a time and a couple of other jobs before starting my business.

Today's kids need to know that the career they choose has

consequences in terms of the lifestyle they will be able to afford. And parents need to understand that their child's 'failure to launch' will become their problem, and can seriously affect their chances of a comfortable retirement.

The cost of living

Today's parents need to be more purposeful than the generation before in setting budgets and introducing our kids to the necessary financial skills, even if we don't practise them ourselves. But know this: if you expect your child to do something at 13 that you are not doing yourself, it is not irony they see, but hypocrisy. This is probably why a number of my clients introduce their teenagers to me with the explanation (in front of their child): 'I haven't done this as well as I should, but I know my kids need to do better than me.' I will then work with them on a one-on-one basis.

Prior to working with a teenager, I ask the parents if I can share information about their own situation. I highlight the strengths and weaknesses of the parents' financial position. I explain what they have done well, and the areas in which they need to improve and that I am working with them on. I have found that teenagers prefer brutal honesty than half-truths, especially when it comes to money discussions.

Kids do well with reality. When given real information, they rise to the occasion. They know if Mum and Dad argue about money and they want to know the reason why. Or they know that Dad works hard but there still doesn't seem to be enough to go around, or that now they get to go on holidays every year but this never used to be the case. They are aware of what other families do, although they are not sure how it relates to their own parents and why they can or cannot do the same. If they are flush, they know this as well. On some level, they may know the money personality of their parents, if they are shoppers or savers.

What they don't usually know, but which is of more relevance, is what their parents earn, what the family spends each year, whether their parents have enough saved for their own retirement, whether they spend everything they earn, the size of their parents' mortgage and when they will be mortgage-free. They might not know some of these things because usually their parents don't know them either! Even if the parents do know this information, in most instances they are not sharing it with their kids. From my observations, the older the parent, the less comfortable they seem to be with this level of transparency.

When speaking with a group of millennials, I asked them what type of lifestyle they wanted to live as adults. For the most part, though some aspired to more, they were comfortable with the level of lifestyle their parents enjoyed. Which then raised the question, well, how much do your parents earn? Only one person could say how much their parents earned, and that was fairly vague. Some had only found out what their parents earned when they were trying to apply for a student allowance.

Most of our kids only find out what we earn when they are ready to leave home. This makes no sense to me and I am pretty quick to dispel this level of ignorance when I work with teenagers.

Firstly, I get them to complete a budget for me of the lifestyle they want to live. I ask them to go home and find out the information from their parents about what things cost, or google it.

Sample budget	Annualised
Accommodation	
Renting (1-bedroom apartment), or	$350 per week
Flatting (budget) or baord	$100–200 per week
Food	
Thrifty shopper (cooks at home, menu planning, looks for specials)	$80 per week
Cooks at home, but likes the odd gourmet recipe	$120 per week
Big spender (visits the supermarket often each week, no menu planning and not looking for specials)	$200 per week
Utilities	
Electricity	$150 per month
Water rates	$50 per month
Internet	$100 per month
Mobile phone	$50 per month
Clothing	
Thrifty, sticks to a budget and only buys at sales	$50 per month
Moderate	$125 per month
Shopaholic, big spender	$500 per month
Vehicle/Transport	
Public transport	$150 per month
Vehicle (petrol, rego, repairs and maintenance, insurance)	$250 per month

Insurance	
Health insurance	$50 per month
Savings and investment	
Bare minimum	$100 per month
Moderate	$200 per month
Retire early	$1000 per month
Discretionary	
Travel	
Visiting family	$250 per year
Annual holiday—local	$500 per year
Overseas	$2500 per year
Eating out/bars/cafés	
Once a week	$50 per week
Twice a week	$150 per week
Often	$250 per week
Hobbies/sports	
Not expensive	$500 per year
Moderate	$1000 per year
Expensive	$3000 per year
Entertainment (movies, concerts, Netflix)	
Not expensive	$100 per month
Moderate	$200 per month
Expensive	$400 per month
Christmas, birthdays and other gifts	
Scrooge McDuck	$300 per annum

Moderate	$800 per year
Generous to a fault	$2000 per year
Donations	
Charity	$50 per month
Tithing (if applicable)	$200 per month

Based on this, an annual amount is tallied up that determines the level of income that needs to be earned for them to live the lifestyle they want.

The takeaway point at this stage is less about how much money they will actually need and more about reinforcing the idea that everything has a cost. The job they eventually take or the career they choose will determine what type of budget they will need to work with. For now we are simply trying to determine if they're going to have champagne tastes on a beer budget, or be more realistic.

I explain that this is their move-out-of-home budget; within a couple of years they will want more from their life, and will probably want to either own a home or have the opportunity to do more things. But money or wealth underpins it all. (Note that if you are going to own your home instead of renting, it may cost you up to $15,000 more per year in extra costs, such as mortgage payments, rates, insurance, repairs, etc.)

So then we look at the career they might be considering—let's find out what it pays. Is it going to 'cut the mustard'?

They will no doubt be passionate about it to start with, but unless that passion can translate to financial opportunity, it will start to die when faced with the realities of wanting to get ahead faster, or their eventual partner wanting more.

It's easy for me to have these conversations because I am the accepted expert in this area. I don't talk to these teenagers as children, I speak to them as adults and show them respect by being honest with them.

When I have tried to encourage parents to do this themselves, it has been met with varying degrees of success. Some teenagers respond well, but most prefer not to hear this information from their parents. The seriousness of the lesson can be lost by who the teacher is.

Identify if you are the right person to have this conversation with your child. If not, ask someone who can speak honestly to these points, who is themselves considered financially successful, and who your teenager will respond to. Whoever gives the lesson, you need to back it up with support and follow-through.

Of course we want our kids to earn enough money to do the things they love. But in reality, many won't. They must design a strategy to grow wealth outside of paid employment as the landscape of career progression and careers in general is transforming.

This is probably the first time you are introducing the concept of sustainability to your kids. You are starting to reinforce the idea that behaviour has consequences. As a parent, you need to be identifying lifestyle and budget shortfalls, and talking about options around money and business to help them dream and realise their goals.

You need to repeat this exercise every year. The detail will become more pertinent and mean more as they get older. Perhaps most importantly, it will highlight the need to consider financial consequences before committing to a career path.

ENTREPRENEURSHIP

Fundamentally, entrepreneurs see solutions where most of us see problems. At its core, entrepreneurship is a mindset, a way of thinking where you imagine new ways to solve a problem, add value and build a profitable business.

A successful entrepreneur tends to be confident and self-motivated. Entrepreneurs are tenacious and tend to have a healthy disrespect for established rules, and set out to do things differently. To them, obstacles and opportunities look the same, and they can turn both to their advantage.

Entrepreneurs share a commitment to turning an idea into a profitable business. Coming up with an idea, although probably the most exciting aspect, is only step one in the journey to becoming an entrepreneur. After the idea, it then needs to be turned into a business. In doing this they organise, develop, manage and assume the risks of a business. This is in fact the hardest part of the process and why a lot of businesses fail, because many people do not have the business knowledge to take their ideas and turn them into profit.

Business skills underpin most successful ventures, so bear this in mind when you are thinking of subjects for your kids to take at school to accompany things they might be more passionate about. More and more of us are becoming self-employed, and this will be an upward trend, as people are feeling safer and more secure about creating their own jobs rather than weathering the uncertainties of economic storms at the perceived whim of employers.

Lawyers, doctors, accountants, writers, actors and other professionals who tend to work as sole practitioners, either contracting to corporates or running their own show, discover quickly that a lack of business skills can undermine the pursuit of a chosen career. I appreciate that you can eventually hire someone who has business acumen, but you need to have enough knowledge to allow you to grow your idea or business to the point where you can afford the employee with the business acumen.

At a young age, you can start to cultivate the entrepreneurial edge in your kids by encouraging them to see opportunity in obstacles. Encourage your kids to identify the things that frustrate them and brainstorm how to fix the problem. This teaches them to focus on positive outcomes and helps them to see that they have the power to change the landscape of life.

You might see entrepreneurial tendencies in your kids from as early as five, although this is rare. It is usually from the ages of 10 to 12 onwards that kids can understand the concept of making money and taking an idea from start to finish.

My first foray into business was when I was aged six. I rounded up the kids in my neighbourhood to put on a play for our parents. We charged $2 per head and served peanuts at intermission.

On reflection, it was probably excruciating for our parents to watch, as we had too many characters in the play for the number of kids involved, which meant that we all had to play two parts each. But this is irrelevant. What is important is that I knew who we were marketing to (our parents), and that they would pay to watch us. Each child made $3 after deducting the costs of the peanuts and props. Popsicles only cost 30 cents at the time, so you can see the value of $3 to us 30 years ago!

A kid's first shot at business usually involves the parents or wider family being the target market. Then it might move to the neighbours or other kids. The most common example of the young budding entrepreneur is the lemonade stand, or the sausage sizzle at the local sports day. Another example I have encouraged is a child having their friends give them their toys and they sell them on TradeMe, clipping the ticket on the sale, or splitting the profits with the friend who gave them the toy. If they are more adventurous, they might research what a toy can be sold for first and then offer to buy the toy from their friend, or at a garage sale, at a cheaper rate, before on-selling it and making a profit.

There are so many opportunities for your kids to learn about money by making money. The trick is to know who you are marketing to and determining what needs to happen to break even.

The most important part of any entrepreneurial activity, whether you are a kid or an adult, is reflecting on what went well and what didn't go so well, what you learned and would change for next time. Failure can be your friend, provided you fail fast. The mastery of this creates self-confidence, self-reliance and the ability to tolerate ordinary frustrations—ironically, the very skill set most employers look for when recruiting.

UNDERSTANDING HOW INTEREST WORKS

Interest rate, yield, annual percentage yield are all different ways of describing the money that a bank or financial institution pays you for keeping your money on deposit with them. It's the money they are prepared to pay for the use of your money, because they take it and invest it themselves or lend it out to someone else.

Teach your kids that the money that sits in a cheque or transactional account should be what is needed to cover your living costs/bills for the month. Any more needs to be invested in a term deposit or something that pays you for the privilege of holding on to your money.

Interest compounds when the bank or financial institution adds interest to your savings at regular intervals and you don't withdraw it, so you start to earn interest on your interest. Compound interest shows the power of time. The longer you leave the money invested, earning interest, the faster the money grows. To start with it is gradual, but then it hits a point where it starts to rocket away.

Show your kids with maths. If you open a savings account with $100 in the bank, and the bank is paying 6 per cent interest, divide the rate by 12 to get the monthly interest rate (so 6 per cent divided by 12 = 0.005, or 0.5 per cent of $100, which is 50 cents per month). Add that to your $100, and at the end of the first month you have $100.50. The next month the bank pays you interest on the new and increased amount of $100.50. At the end of the year you have $106.17 (slightly more than the 6 per cent interest advertised). The 17 cents in this example is not particularly exciting, but if we follow the logic, by the end of five years you will have $134 (instead of $130), and at the end of 10 years you will have $179 (instead of $160). But the real magic happens as your savings balance or the interest rate increases.

Conversely when you have borrowed a lot of money (e.g. a home mortgage) and have to pay it back to the bank, the power of compound interest will be working against you (see chapter 2 for more on this).

Einstein is said to have called compound interest the eighth wonder of the world, and it can be if the interest rate is high enough and the amount of time long enough. However, if the interest rate is so low as to be inconsequential (as it is currently), its power is lost because your savings won't grow fast enough to show any real improvement. As parents, when you are trying to illustrate the benefit of compound interest on savings you might need to top up what the bank pays to create an illustrated rate of at least 6 per cent (ideally 10 per cent), for your child to grasp its benefits.

Compound interest can multiply money almost magically. Compound interest arises when interest is added to the principal, so that, from that point on, the interest that has been added *also* earns interest. This addition of interest to the principal is called compounding.

Let's take a look at an example. If you had $1000 invested at 10 per cent that was compounding every year, then after the first year you would have $1100. This amount is then invested at 10 per cent, meaning you would have $1210. With each year, the amount of interest increases slightly as the amount invested increases, as shown in the graph below.

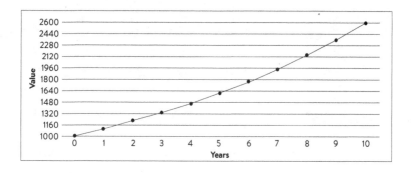

In this example, the interest is calculated annually—or once in a 12-month-period. If the interest was compounded more frequently—say, six-monthly, monthly or daily—the effective interest would be slightly higher as shown in the following table.

Year	Periods	Starting value	Mutiplier	Interest	End value
1	1	$1000.00	10%	$100.00	$1100.00
2	1	$1100.00	10%	$110.00	$1210.00
3	1	$1210.00	10%	$121.00	$1331.00
4	1	$1331.00	10%	$133.10	$1464.10
5	1	$1464.10	10%	$146.10	$1610.51
6	1	$1610.51	10%	$161.05	$1771.56
7	1	$1771.56	10%	$177.16	$1948.72
8	1	$1948.72	10%	$194.87	$2143.59
9	1	$2143.59	10%	$214.36	$2357.95
10	1	$2357.95	10%	$235.79	$2593.74

Here are some example values. Notice that compounding has a very small effect when the interest rate is small, but a large effect for high interest rates.

Compounding	Periods	1.00 %	5.00 %	10.00 %	20.00 %	100.00 %
Yearly	1	1.00 %	5.00 %	10.00 %	20.00 %	100.00 %
Semiannually	2	1.00 %	5.06 %	10.25 %	21.00 %	125.00 %
Quarterly	4	1.00 %	5.09 %	10.38 %	21.55 %	144.14 %
Monthly	12	1.00 %	5.12 %	10.47 %	21.94 %	161.30 %
Daily	365	1.01 %	5.13 %	10.52 %	22.13 %	171.46 %

If you want to work out how fast your money will grow, divide 72 by the annual interest rate and that is how many years it will take for your money to double.

Remind your child that when comparing different investments, you need to consider how often the interest is added to the principal. Compound interest that is added monthly is a better investment than interest which is added once a year (simple interest). The examples above show the difference between monthly interest being earned and annual interest being earned.

While I can show you many examples of compound interest with savings, because the savings interest rate is currently so low, the effect of it is not as exciting. Compound interest is better illustrated with debt. You need to understand this, as it is more likely your child will need to use leverage (debt) to grow their wealth. If they can understand how to use this at the lowest cost, then that is a powerful skill.

CONCLUSION

By the time your child turns 14, you should have determined their money personality, and with this, their opportunities and weaknesses that need to be addressed. They will be receiving an allowance and have practised, individually and with the family, setting and achieving savings goals.

They may be showing entrepreneurial tendencies and need to understand the idea of compound interest. You will soon be introducing how hobbies and passions might not make a career, as well as giving them confidence about how money can be earned, by either working for someone or for yourself.

YOU VALUE THINGS WHEN YOU WORK FOR THEM—TEACHING GRATITUDE

Numerous studies have measured gratitude levels in children and found strong correlations between gratitude and higher grades, level of life satisfaction, and social integration. There is also a link between gratitude and lower levels of envy and depression. Children are grateful when they know they have something that is special. For anything to be special or have value, it can't be a 'given'. It must mean something. Yet helicopter parents keep swooping in to ensure nothing bad happens to their kids when the very idea of something bad happening is what makes you appreciate the good.

So how do you make your kids grateful? What gratitude lessons can you impart as a parent? Wearing my parent hat, I do struggle with this. All too often I will say to my husband that our kids are so ungrateful.

Some believe you should say grace, although less than half of us do this. With fewer people claiming to believe in God, I believe a godless grace still needs to be given —whether it is asking everyone to talk about the highlight of their day, something they appreciate or makes them feel lucky. Toast to it, or give thanks for it. The principle of being grateful exists irrespective of your denomination, or lack thereof.

For our family, daily grace or toasting to our fortune is not part of our ritual, usually because our meal-time routine varies from night to night and whichever parent is in charge. But we try to make a point of discussing the highs and lows of the day. And on our family nights out we speak about the things we are most grateful for (which, for me, is usually an extra five minutes' sleep!). Gratitude is to be encouraged.

CHAPTER 7
14–16: FINANCIAL CHOICES AND CONFIDENCE

The years from 14 to 16 are when you reveal your own financial position and share with your child what you are doing right and wrong, and what you are still working on. This is a confronting chapter in your child's financial development. If these years are navigated correctly, it can be the launching pad towards financial success. If financial education is executed poorly, or not at all, it's likely this will come back to bite both you and your child. 'Failure to launch'—to successfully move into independent adulthood—is one of the most common themes for millennials, and will continue to be for those generations coming after them, unless we do things differently.

Anyone who has raised a moderately talented child understands the financial obligations that often go hand in hand with supporting their talent. Parents often tell me that they will do whatever is needed, wherever possible, to help their kids achieve their potential. It is often the most common non-negotiable item in a family budget. Rarely, though, does this extend to helping their kids become conscious and purposeful about how to meet the financial obligations of funding their talent. Teaching kids to fund their passions prepares them for being able to fund bigger dreams as they mature.

My observation is that parents put so much energy into making a childhood exciting and carefree that they don't always take enough time to prepare their children for an exciting adulthood. I appreciate there is a balance, and an appropriate age to go into some of this detail, but realising your goals as an adult almost always requires economic truths or financial constraints. The ability to confront and overcome these challenges is what sets the successful apart from the rest, and distinguishes the doer from the dreamer.

From age 14 onwards, our kids need to start to be equipped with more economic truths as we start to condition them more purposefully towards independence. You will be needing to share your financial position with them, so if you are not yet on your way to financial independence (in retirement), then I suggest you get a plan in place.

This is the age when you really need to tune in to whether your child is developing the necessary financial skills, intervening if necessary. If you are going to get a financial coach or mentor for your child, from age 15 onwards is the time.

Objectives:
- Learn how to create a budget or spending plan.

- Have an allowance that covers haircuts, mobile phone and clothes.
- Start to understand the relationship between time and money.
- Commit to a savings goal.
- Develop a basic understanding of investment and wealth creation.
- Connect money with the role it plays in their future.
- Start to understand the opportunity cost of spending.
- Be able to read and understand a bank statement.
- Understand where their interests and strengths lie and what career fields these lend themselves to.
- Find out the life costs for the lifestyle they want to live.
- Start to research different jobs and their pay scale.
- Get a part-time job.

Key conversations:
- Talk about why we earn money and how money allows us to live a certain lifestyle.
- Explain how money and happiness are linked.
- Discuss the difference between hobbies and careers.
- Discuss how mastering new skills is necessary to stay relevant in the current age.
- Understand the family finances and discuss whether the parents are on track for retirement.
- Understand the advertising and marketing tactics used to get us to spend more money than we might want to.
- Recognise the need to understand and pursue wealth-creation strategies.

Other developments:
- Start shopping comparatively.
- Get your kid to complete your donation rebate tax return on your behalf.

SPENDING PLAN—INTRODUCING THE BIG GUNS

Some call it a budget, I prefer to call it a spending plan. Basically it's a way of saying, of the money coming in, where do I want it to go? Most adults are a bit useless at this, so I don't know why we expect our kids to do any better. But from the age of 14, your kids need to write down a spending plan.

Some kids will say they don't have any money to necessitate such a plan. But they do, either from a part-time job (which they are about to get), allowances or from pocket money. If they don't, then they need to earn some money so they can learn the lesson of spending.

It's your job to teach them to spend consciously, to make sure that every dollar they spend is connected to making their life tick over or them happier. Too often we spend money on things that don't make us any happier. We spend because we are either not aware we are spending or don't have a reason not to spend.

Encourage your child to project what their income is likely to be for the coming three, six and twelve months, based on their pocket money, allowances, part-time work (if applicable) and gifts (if applicable). Then have them list the things they need to spend money on, i.e. what their allowance has to cover, what they plan to save and give, and what they will have left over for discretionary spending. Soon, we will be more focused on major saving goals (e.g. for a car or university), but for the time being just getting into the zone of having a plan for your spending is a win.

If you have not done so already, increase their allowance to now include haircuts, mobile phone, clothes and sports.

ENCOURAGE REFLECTION AND DISCUSSION AROUND MONEY HANDLING

Check in with them quarterly to see how they are going against their plan. Discuss what they have achieved each quarter, where they have excelled, where they could do better and what the goal is for the next quarter.

Being able to reflect on and discuss money honestly, without emotion, is a huge asset. It helps you to maintain a healthy relationship with money, knowing that you can affect the outcome of your financial decisions. It also assists in relationships when you are an adult. Too often couples fail to discuss money constructively.

A budget tells your money where to go

American author John Maxwell says, 'A budget is telling your money where to go, rather than wondering where it went.' Motivational speaker Zig Ziglar used to say, 'If you aim at nothing, you will hit it every time.'

A spending plan represents intentional living. Why so many people don't budget is because it forces them to acknowledge they are not where they need to be, or doing what they should be doing. It's too confronting, so we opt to do nothing.

I don't care if someone is spending more than they earn or not making the progress that they should—as a financial coach, my job is to identify where they can improve, and to determine the best plan of attack to get them to where they want to be. But getting on any scales (financial or not) can be an embarrassing experience for some, even shameful. My job is to push through this to get people to where they want and need to be.

Save your kids the shame, and show them how to budget. Your job is to watch over them until they prove competency in this area.

With my adult clients, budgeting is a constant challenge that many struggle to manage, as they can't effectively prioritise—and with easy access to credit, they often don't need to. But life will offer both opportunities and curve balls. Your plan needs to be able to withstand these, work with them, exploit opportunity when it's presented and hunker down when curve balls arrive. If you don't live by this mantra, then you are disadvantaging your kids, giving them a distorted sense of financial reality. Remember, while kids are living at home is the safest time for them to fail, as there is a net to catch them and the mistakes are so much smaller.

Once they have got their spending plan down pat, you need to introduce exposure to other family costs. During the last stage, your teen prepared a family dinner, out or in, working to a budget. As they mature we want the level of responsibility to increase. Have your teen plan and budget for a family outing or holiday. You as the parent set the budget. Put the teen in charge of everything that is required for the trip: petrol, food, entry fees and accommodation (where necessary). Encourage them to research the costs. Give them the cash at the start of the day. If they run out of money, then you go home. Do not bail them out. Again, if there is money left over, put it into the 'family treats' jar.

AGE 15: FINANCIAL TRANSPARENCY

From the age of 15, you should be sharing your own financial position with your kids. Explain that it is a measure of respect to them that you share this information, and you expect them to respect your privacy and not pass it on to others. Equally, you need to remind them that if they have any questions, they may ask you.

This will feel revealing, because it is. You need to share with your kids what you earn and what you spend. Whether you own your home and what you pay in mortgage payments. Explain what you have done right and where you have gone wrong. Reflect on your own career path, and who you have met who influenced your behaviour, purchasing choices and asset purchases.

Show your kids your pay slip. (Some parents are afraid of doing this, but if your kids want to know what you are paid, they can just google it, and probably have—so don't be too concerned or sensitive about it.)This may be the first time your child has seen a pay slip, and certainly one with an amount as big as yours on it. Show them how much of the money you earn is deducted for tax, what is going towards KiwiSaver and what you have left.

Take the time to discuss how much tax is paid and why it is paid. Start the conversation around what tax covers: roads, police, hospitals, teachers, libraries, those less fortunate.

If you can, use real money to illustrate this. If you can't, then use play money. But calculate how much money is coming in and put this in a pile on the table. Then take out 10 per cent that should be put towards retirement or faster mortgage repayment.

Next, list all your fixed costs: costs you incur each week or month, costs you can't argue over or choose not to pay. For example: mortgage or rent, home maintenance, rates, food, internet, power, alarm, insurance, phone, petrol, medical. Get your kid to write down what they think each item will cost per month, and compare it with the actual amounts.

Now, using the pile of money in the middle of the table, get them to count out the amount required to cover fixed costs from the available money pile. They will see the pile of money left over getting smaller and smaller. If you have started this journey when your kids were young, this will not be the first time you have illustrated the money coming in and out in order to fund the family. But it will be the first time your child will be able to connect income earned with progress achieved, or not.

The amounts do not need to be exact. This is only an illustration of money used each month. The small pile left over is your discretionary pile. Explain that there will be some things that the family wants to spend money on, for example, sports, a family holiday or a cleaner. Factor in the monthly equivalent of that cost. Then show them what is left over.

WHAT IF YOU KNOW YOU HAVEN'T DONE IT RIGHT?

The best time to plant an oak tree was 20 years ago. The second best time is now.

It doesn't matter if your financial situation is dire, if you wish you had done things differently, or if you feel you have left your run too late to sort your finances. It is never too late to start, because any improvement, however small, is still an improvement. Your children will catch on to this effort and it will send a strong message their way, especially if it is accompanied by some real honesty around what you could have done better and what you would wish for your child.

MONEY AND HAPPINESS

Nothing more directly affects your happiness than money. Sure, happiness is about all the things money can't buy: health, love respect, all of which are determined by who you are, not what you have. But the kind of happiness I am talking about is your quality of life: to be able to live life to its fullest potential; to be able to afford and enjoy the pursuits you are most passionate about.

I am all for authentic happiness. But it is a lie not to acknowledge that money plays a pivotal role in this. Perhaps this is why so many are disconnected from their money, because no one is prepared to call them on the fact that money makes the world go around.

Money allows you to pay for care for your children if they need an operation. Money allows you to give up your job to help your parents as they age, or to live in a safe neighbourhood so your kids can go to a good school. If you don't buy into the role money plays in creating happiness, you don't give it the respect it deserves, which will surely lead to unhappiness or a degree of financial stress from not being in control of your money.

Financial stress underpins a lot of broken relationships and creates a lot of miscommunication. It leads to absenteeism and being unproductive at work. It is the leading cause of insomnia in females and a source of anxiety for many, especially as they start to get older.

The solution for a lot of people when trying to combat financial stress is to earn more money. But, unless there is an improved system behind them doing better, then the more money that comes in, the more money goes out—and the whole exercise is in vain. Many of my clients are not in a position to earn more money, so we have to work with what they have.

Money isn't a dirty word. Money underpins opportunity.

Opportunity and progress lead to happiness, and being happy is the result that most of us strive for. Money is a commodity that our kids need to master; they need to learn that doing well with money is something to be respected, not scoffed at.

START TALKING ABOUT CAREERS

This is the age that your kids are having to think about what career they might be interested in, and the subjects they may need to take to train for that career. Few kids have any clue about their career options at this point, but you can help paint a financial reality for them.

This is where you may want to involve some outside help. Revisit the sample living budget you introduced to them when they were 13 (see chapter 6), as it will start to have more relevance, and mean more now. Get them to read the weekend papers, or look online, to see what jobs are on offer, and what they are paying. Start to bring the future closer to them. Discuss the different jobs with them to help them understand their function and what qualifications may be needed.

If your kid has no clue about what they want to be, it is likely they will default to what they are good at or passionate about—which is a good starting point, although the cynic in me questions whether a 16-year-old actually knows their passions. For some reason, there is a huge push in society today to find a job that you are passionate about, otherwise, we are told (probably by Facebook), your life will not be fulfilled. The essence of this is honourable, but the actual interpretation is dangerously flawed. However, many teenagers buy into the rhetoric without understanding the meaning.

I saw this in action when I interviewed some Year 12 students and asked how they were going to decide what they wanted to do when they left school. They went on about doing something they are passionate about (snore). They also went on about wanting to work smarter, not harder. They interpreted working smarter as not having to work as hard. I explained that working smarter was still working just as hard but you had more output for your input, as opposed to putting in less effort—a subtle yet significant interpretational flaw.

These students have been told by the media, and possibly their parents and their friends, that to live a fulfilled life you must do something you are passionate about. But let's look deeper. Most things we love don't enable us to make money or at least enough money to facilitate the lifestyle we want to live. If you can make your passions sufficiently profitable, then of course this can work. But without a consideration of the financial implications, following your heart without a reality check is more likely to create a whole lot of pain.

Finding your *ikigai*

The concept of fulfilment is better described by the Japanese word *ikigai*. When you have an *ikigai*, you have 'a reason to get up in the morning', something that makes life worth living. A *raison d'être* (literally: reason for being). Passion is only one part of finding your *ikigai*. In addition to doing what you love and are good at, you must also determine whether there is a need for your skill and a desire for someone to pay you enough to sustain you at the expense of other opportunities.

Your *ikigai* is at the centre of the interconnecting circles. Your *ikigai* does not mean one thing that satisfies all parts of your life or each interconnected layer in the diagram. Instead, it lists the most common areas you find its components working

in harmony, between work, children and hobbies. Which makes sense, right? Certainly, some of us will be lucky enough to find a job that provides what the world needs, which we can be paid for, that we are both passionate about and good at. But these jobs are hard to find, and I would certainly not expect to find them lurking at the bottom of the ladder where a school-leaver or graduate will be starting. It baffles me that we would encourage our kids to follow their passions without also giving them a healthy dose of reality.

A lot of the millennials that I speak to seem to be drifting through life in search of their *ikigai*. Let's face it, who isn't? They are looking for a reason to get up in the morning, but not surprisingly, few, if any, have found it. And those who couldn't find their reason to get up out of bed in the morning usually opted to sleep in till lunch.

Yes, acknowledge what your child is passionate about and

good at. Can that lead to a job that pays them, or a business proposition? Will it pay them enough for the life they want to live? What skills lurk under the surface of their passion that could be transferrable to another job or career? Help your kids dig deeper and brainstorm options. But keep bringing it back to what they need to earn to live a life they enjoy. Money is not a dirty word. It's simply a commodity.

As I expected, when I interviewed school-leavers, for the most part they were choosing a tertiary study course based on what they were either good at or passionate about. Few had considered the financial implication of their career choice and how they could substitute what was likely to be a low income with other initiatives. One girl (who was particularly lovely) said she wanted to do performing arts at university. I asked how much she thought she would make as a graduate in this field. She said she knew it was particularly poorly paid, but she was passionate about it so she was going to do it. I asked her who had encouraged her in this field. She said that no one had encouraged her as such, but no one had dissuaded her. I asked what her school's career advisor had had to say about it, and she said that he reiterated that doing something you are passionate about is important.

In my experience, passion about anything is lost quickly if it prevents you living the life you or your family want and enjoy. Because this girl didn't know what the lifestyle she wanted would cost, it was a fairly pointless argument. Which brings me to my next point: how do you even know what you are passionate about at 17, when your exposure to life is limited and usually Facebook-filtered?

When I interviewed millennials, they were less prepared to work unless they were passionate about the job. I mean, who is passionate about any job, especially when they are starting at the bottom of the food chain?

If there was no cost to explore your passions and options, then you could fill your boots. But there is a cost. There is a literal cost (tertiary education) and an opportunity cost. No one seems to be telling these kids that self-actualisation doesn't tend to occur at 20. Don't you have to have experienced the wrongs of life to find your right?

While it would be amazing to have a vocation, or to do something you are passionate about, the world doesn't really work like this. Well, not when you are 17. You have to find your *ikigai*—and it usually doesn't lie with you doing something you love or are passionate about in isolation.

Unfortunately, most passions are likely to remain a hobby only. Hobbies seldom replace a job. If you can make money from it, great. If you can make an income from it, awesome. It's possible, certainly. But probable? No, and it's even less likely that you can turn a hobby into a profitable job at 17.

Of course, we all want to love what we do, but just as important to what you do in your job is the environment that you work in, the people you work with and the cause that you stand for. In fact, the latter can affect your job satisfaction more than the task at hand.

In the case of the performing arts student, if I was coaching her on some life strategies, I would want her to first complete a budget of what her lifestyle is likely to cost when she finishes her studies. I would want to know her course costs and the likely size of her student loan. I would have her research the job prospects available and the likely pay range she would earn. Is there a shortfall between what she needs to live and what she is likely to earn?

If there is a shortfall, we wouldn't hide from the fact. We would own it, and work through all the alternatives available to bridge the gap. I would say, be what you want to be, but don't be ignorant about what it will mean to follow your dreams. I would introduce her to various people in the industry that she wants to work in so she could get a flavour of what her likely career will look and feel like in its daily grind. We would consider business ideas, moving overseas, working a second job and ways to minimise her student loan. The range of things that can be done to balance out a low-paying career is extensive. The lower the salary, the more creative and sometimes aggressive you need to be to ensure you can still live a life you enjoy.

Hobbies versus work

The problem with Facebook and your general online presence is that the cookies created generate your own individual and insular ecosystem that can disconnect you from reality. The very notion of *ikigai* is that it is grounded in reality. Instead of creating a balanced view challenged by the opposing arguments, extreme views are left unchallenged, and our kids and their 'feeds' play to this, reiterating what they believe to be true, when it might not be.

I have seen parents overindulge their children's hobbies to the point of the child thinking they have a future in it, and maybe for a short amount of time they do. But a hobby is just a hobby. Even if you are good at it, that doesn't mean it is going to translate to you earning enough money to live the lifestyle you are familiar with. Parents need to temper their children's desires with reality.

Too often, too little consideration is given to the equally important *ikigai* principle of 'that which you can be paid for'—

and whether that will be sufficient to cover the rest of your life's costs.

Of course you need to do things in life that you are passionate about. You also need to do things that earn you money, and are consistent with your own values. If you can blend them together, then you can create your dream role. But if that dream role is working with people you don't like in an industry you don't enjoy then it will no longer be your dream role. Or if the dream role requires you to freelance but you don't like doing administration or accounts, then it's no longer so perfect.

Tell your kids: don't aim for perfection—it's an illusion. Accept that it is hard to find a job that creates self-actualisation while paying you. Also realise that it is possible to move towards your dream role but you usually have to create wealth in order to facilitate this. And wealth creation takes time and leverage (discussed in the next chapter).

IT'S TIME TO GET TO WORK ... LITERALLY

While I am offending people left right and centre, let's continue as we mean to go on! From the age of 15 or 16 you need to encourage your child to get a part-time job.

British financial educator Joline Godfrey, in her book *Raising Financially Fit Kids*, says she believes children from families on all income levels who master work experiences have a greater self-confidence and sense of self-worth than those whose primary activity has been to satisfy themselves or consume. She found in her 30 years of working with kids that those who start early have an easier time mastering the skills than kids who aren't required to work for pay until university or later. 'Connecting work with earning money is valuable in developing responsible work habits, acquiring discipline and understanding the need to make hard choices.' It develops emotional and adaptable intelligence (EQ and AQ), which is considered just as important to employers as school grades.

What our kids learn from employment is a work ethic. This phrase covers the ability to listen, exert ourselves, cooperate with others, do our best and stick to a task until we have finished it and done it right. More recently, work ethic has been described as 'grit', a term made popular by Angela Duckworth of the University of Pennsylvania.

Grit is a quality any top athlete and entrepreneur embodies. Grit is what sets two equally smart people apart from each other. Duckworth says grit distinguishes itself from the general tendency to be reliable or self-controlled. It's about long-term stamina rather than short-term intensity. A lot of my clients need grit in order to move from being on the back foot financially. Financial grit is about being able to live a life you enjoy without compromising the future. It's a form of emotional intelligence and will always be more of an indicator of financial success than your IQ score or your level of financial literacy.

This is what part-time work teaches kids. Plus, a job involving menial tasks highlights the importance of not staying in that position for the rest of your life. All the jobs I did while at school confirmed to me that I never wanted to do them as my real job. I delivered papers, and worked on an orchard thinning apples. I thought I would love working outside in the sun. I thought I would like to get fit while earning money. (The concept still sounds great.) But for me, the reality didn't match the romance of it. Instead of focusing on how toned I was becoming, all I focused on was being hot and sweaty all day, and the shorts marks that were ruining my tan-line. It was back-breaking work, up and down ladders all day. My fingers got blisters. I dreamt of apples and got sick of listening to music for eight hours straight.

On the job, I had the option of working for an hourly rate or on contract (where I was paid on a per-tree thinned and completed basis). I preferred to be paid for what I did. Hard workers usually do. The best reflection of this as an adult is being your own boss, or working in sales, where any extra effort you make benefits you as the owner of the business (in theory at least) or the receiver of commission. I was motivated to do more when I was rewarded with more.

Working for someone who is not your parent, who expects you to show up and perform and is not interested in anything else, is an invaluable experience. In working for an employer, your child will start to understand how life works outside the home, and how the principles of commerce mean that people need to show up and do their best, otherwise there are others who are happy to replace them. Most importantly, experience of work leads to more discussion around how income can be derived, which is a principle of wealth creation. If you want to impress a prospective employer that you have the right attitude, nothing says it better than having had a menial job that you stuck at.

John Cowan of The Parenting Place agrees that work creates a link between compliance and responsibility. 'Being able to offer a degree of obedience and compliance is really important—otherwise, if you're not teaching them that, what you're getting at 15 is a tantrum of "but I want it, and I have to have it now".'

In spite of clear evidence that working between 10 and 15 hours per week while at school (and later, at university—see chapter 10) does not disadvantage your child, and can in fact improve their grades, many parents still do not require their teenager to work. This is usually because they have so many other things in their days and in their weekends—which as a parent you need to balance. If your child is wanting a car or likely to get a student loan, then they need to be earning money to minimise these costs. In addition to this, future employers consider the workplace experience your child has had as a way of differentiating them from all the other degree-holders they are competing against. If that job can teach your child teamwork in a work setting, client relationship skills and how good leaders operate, these are the skills employers are looking for. When recruiting staff, attitude and willingness to learn play a huge part. If your child can get the inside edge over someone else, and become better at prioritising because they have less spare time, as well as appreciating the money earned and saving faster for their future—well, I am struggling to see how this could be a bad thing.

Please don't tell me your child is so busy they can't find 10 hours of their time each week to work—because I will not believe you. Certainly their days may be full with extra-curricular activities, but how about you switch out one for another, and for one that pays? Team sports are great, but working develops skills beyond what are demonstrated within a sports team. That is not to say that team sport is not important, because it is. It develops a commitment to a team, to show up each time, even when you don't want to. To work together for a greater outcome, to manage team dynamics. All good stuff. But at the end of the day you are doing something you love. And most of us find it easier to do something we love than something we need to do. Life is not always about doing what you love. Being able to do something you don't love, and still show up—well, that shows gumption.

OPPORTUNITY COST

Opportunity cost is one of those fancy terms that some people never grasp. The idea is if you spend money on something today, you don't have the money that has been spent available to buy something else. This is a concept that I see parents undermine their kids' learning around, because they give them the money so they can buy the thing they want today *and* the thing they want tomorrow.

You need to start introducing the concept of choice and opportunity cost as young as five. You are teaching them to make informed decisions around what they want, and what they will miss out on because of what they want. This means that not only is there a cost to buy something now—being what you pay— but there is a cost (that you don't pay money for) because you then can't buy something else because you have already spent the money. For example: I bought a handbag for $300. The monetary cost was $300, but because I bought that handbag, I did not have any money left over to buy a pair of shoes. So not only did the handbag cost me $300, it also cost the opportunity of being able to buy some shoes.

In my business, we discuss the opportunity cost of every large-expense item. What are we not able to do because we are doing this? Teach your children the same concept, especially while funds are limited and they do not have access to credit. As soon as debt is introduced, they are tempted to no longer choose, and instead do both. This will set them up for a world of pain and financial ineptitude.

Use an example they care about. 'If you buy this album today, you won't have the money to buy the new one that comes out next month.' As human beings, we know that it is hard for most of us to weigh the value of future happiness against the immediate thrill of buying something now, but understanding the opportunity cost of something is at least bringing some consciousness to the decision being made.

SAVING FOR THE FUTURE

The two most common major financial goals for teenagers are buying a car and saving for university or other tertiary study.

One of the first big purchases your child will make will be a car. From the ages of 14 to 16 this will probably be the thing they will be focusing on.

Encourage this. Do not buy them a new car. Do not give them your car. Let them learn to save, to delay reward for a future purchase. Contribute to the car if you must, but don't steal one of their most rewarding purchases from them, even if their friends' parents are doing the opposite.

If they are not fussed on a car, then encourage them to save for university. Their goal should be to save the first semester's worth of university fees as a minimum, but ideally the first year's fees (excluding living costs).

BUYING DEFENCE—TEACHING YOUR KIDS ABOUT MARKETING

According to some American studies, in 1985, children aged four to 12 influenced US$50 billion of their parents' purchases every year. By 2000 that figure had quadrupled to over $200 billion, and it keeps on increasing at a rate of $30–$50 million every five years. Kids are targets because companies are well aware that a nagging child can wear down a parent's resolve more effectively than an ad campaign targeting the parents.

We live in the most marketed-to culture in the history of the world. We are hit by more advertising impressions in a few hours than previous generations experienced in an entire year.

So much of communication and decision-making occurs at the subconscious level, requiring marketers to consider the psychological underpinnings of consumer behaviour. Teach your kids some of the marketing tricks of the trade, so they don't become a fatality to consumerism. In order to arm them against businesses trying to separate them from their money, teach your kids some of the more obvious points of marketing psychology 101:

- anchoring
- persuasion
- decoy effect
- reciprocity
- priming
- celebrity endorsements
- payment options.

Anchoring

Anchoring refers to the tendency to rely heavily on the first piece of information presented when making decisions. Salespeople often place premium products next to standard options to create a sense of value. One common anchoring technique is price anchoring. This is when you compare the price of a product to another, more expensive product: 'Similar products sell for $100–$150, but you can get this product for $70.' This anchors the price to $150 and gives the perception of a 'deal' by offering the product at a lower than expected price.

Persuasion

Persuasion applies to the promotions aspect of the marketing mix, and builds on a customer's impulsive behaviour to lead them to making a purchase. If you look at a website, persuasive marketing includes the layout, look and feel, and user experience that leads a customer to buy. It is about how information is presented to the consumer.

Decoy effect

When faced with a third choice, a strategically placed decoy, customers will more likely choose the more expensive of the other two options. The decoy is priced close to the more expensive options, suggesting that the more expensive option is better. Without a decoy, customers would normally opt for the cheaper option.

The most profound use of the decoy effect is often seen on online pricing pages, where subscribers can be offered three options, with the middle price option so close to the most expensive option that you can't help but spend more due to the added extras at a fraction more of the price. Jeremy Smith of Warwick University wrote an aticle on how to use the decoy effect to help buyers choose the right option, giving the example of magazine *The Economist* and its decoy-pricing model.

The Economist provided three options for subscribers—a digital subscription, a print subscription, and a print plus digital subscription. It looked like this (minus the headline):

The Decoy Effect in Action

Economist.com Subscription	Economist Print Subscription	Economist.com + Economist Print Subscription
$59	$125	$125

Who wouldn't choose the double option? More value, right? If you can get the print edition for $125, plus the digital, then why would you only get the print edition for the same price?

It makes no sense! It's stupid not to choose that third option. Right?

Ah, but who's being duped by whom? *The Economist* is not being stupid. They are being savvy. They know that the offer looks dumb—two unequal options being sold for the same price. But they also know what the decoy (the middle option) is going to do. It's going to make you focus on the awesomeness of the third option.

But take away the decoy, and what do you get?

The Decoy Effect in Action

Economist.com Subscription	Economist Print Subscription
$59	$125

You have two options with a huge price disparity. The $59 edition is obviously far cheaper but you get the same content. Might as well pay $59 instead of $125! This is the power of the decoy.

Reciprocity

Reciprocity is a social psychology rule that says people should repay, in kind, what they receive. We give back the same treatment we receive. If you receive a gift from someone, you often feel obliged to repay them with a gift.

In the marketing world, businesses seem to offer something to consumers for free, to make them feel indebted. This is often used in content marketing or blogging, which gives away something of value for free in the form of posts. Free trials or e-book samples are other examples of this marketing strategy.

To amplify the effects of reciprocity the business will try to incite the feeling of indebtedness in you by offering something to you first, before you buy from them.

Priming

Priming is where subtle suggestions are made to the subconscious mind that can influence subsequent behaviour. It 'primes' the customer for a message or marketing pitch. For example, grocery stores display flowers out front in order to prime customers with an image of freshness. In terms of a website, it might mean using colour schemes or visual imagery to improve a visitor's response to the website.

Celebrity endorsement

It is common in advertising to use people or brands to tell a story as to why you should buy something. The Kardashians are the millennial version of this, and they do it well. It's a typical marketing technique that has merit.

However, when it comes to wealth creation, you can't be influenced by famous faces. Anything to do with finance or an investment needs to stand on its own two feet and you have to encourage your children to look beyond the famous face to the actual investment. They can follow the crowds with all other discretionary purchases if they must—but not investment.

When it comes to investing money, you need to understand the mechanics behind what makes money grow and teach your children these principles, so they don't become a victim of naivety. In the last GFC, a number of finance companies went under. They went under because their investments were not sound, despite the famous faces that endorsed them.

Payment options

Many businesses offer payment plans at 0 per cent interest, but charge an admin fee for the privilege of the arrangement. Check all the hidden costs in deciding to pay something off to make sure the total cost you are paying is justified for the goods purchased.

After explaining the different concepts, get your kids to start spotting the techniques in action. Wise them up to how advertising works and how they can double outsmart it.

One of the most effective buying defences you can apply is universal: sleep on it. As parents, you need to practise this as well. Show your kids that waiting overnight can take the pressure off a decision. This gives you permission to clear your head before you spend the money.

In theory this can work, but when you are super-busy, you might undermine the intent of this with the reality that you are time-poor and you need to get things done. I get it, and do it myself. Just be mindful of overspending and then regretting the purchase.

Human quirks and emotions have a profound impact on economic decisions. A tonne of feelings are tied up in the decisions we make about our money and the amount we earn and have at any given moment. Learning to recognise and control these emotions is the most important factor in picking the right investment (and future partner). It is our feelings that drive bad behaviour and lousy decision-making. People are not dispassionate about money, nor are they rational and calm about their kids. Money is an emotional topic, linked to our self-worth, self-esteem and general wellbeing. Show your kids how you can discuss it rationally.

GOAL SETTING—THE SUBTLETY OF RE-ENGAGING GOALS

Most of us are lazy or busy. This means that in the absence of a clear goal, we tend to drift along. I see this time and time again with clients who are financially aimless or lacking a plan. They just float. As the saying goes, 'the poorest of all men is not the man without a cent but the man without a vision'. And being aimless seems to be exacerbated during adolescence.

The biggest difference between those who achieve their goals and those who don't is that the achievers write down their goals, visualise them and review them often. After you have determined the goal, you need to be considering the obstacles. Believing in a vision requires you to consider all obstacles. Your ability to immerse yourself in the dissenting view is the fastest way of evolving your strategy.

For a goal to be achievable, you need to be able to see that the objective is possible. You need to be able to visualise it. If you can't visualise it or imagine it, then the risk is that you subconsciously don't believe it is possible.

But this is the wrong conclusion. It may not be that it isn't possible, but that you need someone to help you articulate the end goal and how you are going to get there, for you to believe in the goal itself.

Too many people (my clients included) want to get ahead financially and have a loose goal about this. But they don't have a plan or strategy to get there, so the goal remains too far removed. Many of us work with professionals to help us achieve our goals, whether it is weight loss, sports excellence, business improvement or personal development. We need to be open to doing this with our finances, especially as we look down the barrel of the future, when our goals will be further away and we have less time to get there. While many people are OK with getting support to help them achieve the things they are passionate about, they seem to be less accepting of setting goals and making progress to overcome setbacks, especially financial ones.

Research has shown that two factors significantly influence a person's ability to achieve a goal: challenge and ability. People need to feel sufficiently challenged, to contribute to the feeling of accomplishment once the goal has been reached. But there must be a realistic possibility the goal will in fact be attained. If the goal-setter does not believe it is doable, then they disengage.

For long-term goals (which financial goals tend to be), you must keep reconnecting with the goal over time. When it comes to having to sustain or reconnect with goals, people are more likely to re-engage with a goal that has a high–low range instead

HOW TO NEGOTIATE—PUTTING THE D IN DISCOUNT

When you model for your child how to negotiate, you are teaching them to face conflict. Negotiating price is a type of conflict. Teaching a child to enter a negotiation with a win–win spirit teaches them to fight to get the best deal.

I have always found it hard to ask for a discount; the idea of negotiating can be intimidating. But the odds are that your kids will need to negotiate for something important at some stage in their life (usually a pay rise or a property purchase), so if you can teach them some basics now it will go a long way. When negotiating, you need to follow these rules.

1. Do your homework. Understand what competitors charge, what margins are being made, if the seller is facing a deadline, and the reason they are selling.
2. Make the other person name their price first. Michael Soon Lee, author of *Black Belt Negotiating*, is adamant on this point. He says naming a price first limits how low you can go, even if you are trying to establish a low anchor.
3. Know your limit as to how much you can spend.
4. Know when to be quiet, when to be reasonable and when to walk away.
5. Ask for extras, as this might be easier than a discount for the seller to provide.
6. Always ask what discount will apply if you pay cash.
7. Be prepared to walk away. This is potentially the most powerful tactic you have.

of a specific target, according to research by Maura Scott and Stephen Nowlis in the US. For example, instead of setting a goal of saving $1000 every three months, to keep you re-engaged, set the goal to be to save between $900 and $1000. The subtle difference in the goal allows ongoing financial progress to become more sustainable.

Our kids need to be challenged with the financial goals that they set, but they also need to have a sense that they can actually achieve their goals. If breaking a goal down into smaller chunks doesn't engage them, try to motivate them with a range, from high to low, of what to aim for instead of a specific target. Ultimately you need to keep them moving forward.

WEALTH CREATION—SOWING THE SEEDS

Income can be derived actively or passively. Active income means you are working hours for dollars, either doing this via employment or on contract (as a freelancer). Being a freelancer or a contractor is technically being self-employed, although self-employment in my view is more about managing a business or an operation, something more than charging someone an hourly rate. When you operate a business (in the purest sense of the word), it is an opportunity to earn more than a charge-out rate: it has growth potential and the ability to recruit staff to earn more money. That said, whether you work for yourself or someone else, in whatever capacity, you are still having to work. You are still active.

Unlike working, wealth creation is passive income. It's when you take the income you earn and invest it make you more money.

To create wealth, you must first have income left over once you have paid for your living expenses. We will call this your cash surplus. A cash surplus allows you to create wealth, which you do from business activities (rent or dividends/drawings from your business), or portfolio income such as dividends, interest, capital gains and royalties.

The goal is to create passive income, especially by retirement, but many people are not sure what route to take. There is too much information available about the different options and for many this leads to the wrong route or no route being travelled.

As discussed earlier, a lot of kids are choosing careers that will mean the income that they earn will be capped and unlikely to be at a level for them to enjoy the lifestyle they are either accustomed to, or want to live. This shortfall in income can be offset with wealth, but they will need to understand the concept of wealth creation to put it in place while their living costs are low.

The most common wealth-creation strategy (in New Zealand at least) is KiwiSaver, then property investment. KiwiSaver is passive and so is property investment to an extent, but you usually do need to be involved in some of the decisions and actions around the property, which can make it more active than you might want.

CONCLUSION

Your job as a parent is to help your child to identify the financial realities of their career choice, and to determine if additional wealth-creation strategies are going to be necessary in order for them to lead a comfortable life. You also need to take the time to educate them about their options, so that they appreciate that Door A may lead to their career of choice but come with certain financial responsibilities attached, while Door B might be their less-preferred career but not require additional wealth-creation strategies.

CHAPTER 8
16–18: TRANSITIONING INTO ADULTHOOD

The results of two recent US studies of the money attitudes, behaviour and expectations of 16–18-year-olds are fascinating. Firstly, teens say that the money issues of their generation are different from those of their parents. It's easier to spend money and the financial choices are tougher. The majority believe that university is more expensive, and there is more pressure to have more things like computers, cell phones and clothes. The majority believe it is harder for them to get jobs than in their parents' day, although 59 per cent remain optimistic that they will do better than their parents financially.

Teens claim to be more experienced than previous generations about shopping for the best deal when making a purchase, to know the difference between debit and credit cards and how to budget. Yet a chunk of those surveyed aren't savvy about important specifics like what a credit score is, how credit-card interest and fees are incurred or how taxes work. Despite their increased optimism, most believe they will rely on their parents' support for a longer period (hmmmm). Most students believe they are borrowing too much to pay for a university education, and while they are likely to have discussed it with their family, they are unsure about how much they will need to borrow, or how long it will take to repay.

On a positive note, a whopping 86 per cent want to learn about money and how to not make mistakes in the real world, although in my research, who they learn from has as much relevance as the lesson being taught. The teenagers I spoke to said that they don't see it as their school's responsibility, and they might not always listen to their parents, but they are willing to hear the lesson.

We see this play out as adults. So many of the 'hard conversations' need to be had by the right person at the right time to be taken on board in the right way. This is why most of us prefer someone qualified and independent commenting on our finances, as it removes the emotional element of the discussion.

Objectives:
- Understand the options available to grow wealth.
- Be able to read a company's financial statements.
- Determine if they want to work for someone else or for themselves.
- Understand how leverage works.
- Start to understand the relationship between time and money as it relates to debt.
- Understand what taxes are paid for.
- Understand how the banking system works and what caused the Global Financial Crisis.

- Understand the due diligence process and why it is needed.
- Understand good debt versus bad debt.

Key conversations:
- Discuss how women are more exposed financially than men are.
- Discuss what employers are looking for.
- If they are going to complete tertiary study after school, discuss what will it cost, how will they be paid and the wider implications of debt.
- Discuss credit cards and how to use them properly.
- What does being self-employed entail?
- What are the habits of successful and effective people?

Other developments:
- Kids need role models to help them through this stage.
- Introduce them to your 'team', who help you be the best you can be.
- You may need to invest in career advice for your kids.
- Introduce your child to someone who is successfully self-employed (their own boss), in an industry of interest to your child.
- Only pay for your kids' university education if you have your own retirement sorted.

AGE 16—FINANCIAL SNAPSHOT

By the time your child is 16, they should be able to demonstrate earning money with a part-time job and have knowledge and experience of saving, spending and investing. They need to associate money with independence and be transitioning to self-sufficiency.

Without a doubt, young people who have not learned to save, spend wisely, invest and handle debt with self-awareness, and act generously are more likely to have trouble leaving the nest, to accrue debt after high school and have trouble curbing their impulses to spend or have something immediately (especially if they are a shopper by nature). These kids are likely to spend up to 10 years after finishing school living at home.

From age 16 onwards, you are consciously shifting financial reliance from you as parents to your kids. This is when the family budget is revealed in detail. If you don't have one—like most Kiwi families don't—then make one.

The older the person I speak to, the more they believe that the details of the family finances should be kept private. Personally, I strongly disagree. Our kids are making some of the biggest financial decisions of their lives at 17 years old. They are making these decisions against the backdrop of their financial knowledge, which is sketchy at best, usually caught not taught, and with no real idea what life costs. As discussed previously, the earliest that this should be revealed is 14 or 15, but in most cases 16 or 17 is more realistic.

This is also the time that you introduce your child to someone who has had to strive to be successful, who has failed and still moved on to success. Let them speak to your child about this experience and what they have learned. If you have personal experiences of financial failure and how you overcame the setback, then now is the time to share. Making a mistake and then recovering is one of the greatest gifts you can give your child. The years between 16 and 18 are the time to give teens the opportunity to take risks and make mistakes. When a mistake happens, it's not about analysing what they did wrong, but instead understanding what they have learned from it.

This is the time to water the seed that income alone is going to be insufficient to allow them to live a comfortable lifestyle as they get older. They will need to combine this with investment and an understanding of leverage. The purpose of discussing investments is to open their eyes to the possibility of wealth creation. They need to understand KiwiSaver, but also recognise that while it's a great scheme, it is going to be unlikely to provide for their retirement in full, so they need some strategies to bridge the retirement gap. Few of the school-leavers I spoke to had any real grasp of these concepts.

QUESTIONS TEENS SHOULD ASK THEIR PARENTS

When I am coaching teenagers about getting in control of their money, I have them interview their parents, who aren't always my clients. I ask them to find out the answers to the following questions:

- Who taught you about money?
- What do you think your money personality is? Have you always been that way?
- What have you done about providing for your retirement?
- When are you going to be mortgage-free?
- How much do you save?
- Do you increase your savings as you earn more?
- If you could do things differently, what would you do?

How do you expect your children to get ahead and respect money if your behaviour doesn't align with the message? If you want to instil a different outlook and behaviour in your kids, you have to show that you are prepared to take things more seriously. If you don't know the answers to some of these questions, find out.

WEALTH CREATION AND HOW IT WORKS

More on compound interest

One of the greatest misconceptions about investing is that it takes a lot of money to make a lot of money. This is not the case. What it takes is some money and a lot of time. Time is a crucial component of investment, but that is where we tend to disadvantage ourselves.

Let's look at two different scenarios.

Natalie starts to save for her retirement at 25. Tim starts to save at 45. They both commit to saving $200 per month and will earn an average annual return on their investment of 8 per cent. (This doesn't mean that they will earn 8 per cent every year, but that over many years their gains and losses will work out to be an average return of 8 per cent.)

By the time Natalie is 45 years old, she has invested $48,000 of her own money and it has grown to nearly $119,000. Tim hasn't started saving by this point.

From the age of 45 to 65, Natalie keeps up her investment plan and Tim finally starts his. When they hit 65, Natalie has been saving for 40 years and has invested $96,000. Tim started later, has only invested for 20 years and has invested $48,000. But look at the total value of the fund:

At aged 65	Natalie	Tim
Amount invested	$96,000	$48,000
Total Value	$702,856	$118,589

Apart from the difference in invested amount the next remaining difference between the two is time. If Tim was going to end up with the same amount as Natalie, he would have to contribute $1200 per month from the age of 45, paying a whopping $192,000 more than Natalie over his lifetime to end up at the same end value.

As I touched on in the previous chapter, this phenomenon is known as compound interest. When your interest is added to the original investment and the new combined amount, then gets interest on the combined total, that then increases the combined total and gets interest on the higher amount. It builds like a snowball, increasing a little more each year. Although saving the principal makes sense, practically the returns need to be good and the money invested for a long time for the magic of compound interest to kick in. Bank interest rates currently do not cut the mustard for compound interest to be close to motivating, so you need to look beyond the bank rates, to other investment options like bonds, shares and KiwiSaver, with a preference for KiwiSaver.

Natalie's nest egg is almost six times bigger than Tim's. She has invested $48,000 more, but ends up with $585,000 more. The only difference between the two is time.

The same principle is used against you with your home mortgage: the longer you have it, the more it will cost you. In many cases, almost three times the amount you borrowed ends up getting repaid to the bank.

Some millennials I interviewed would say therefore there is no point owning your own home and they see no value in it. To which I say, you have to live somewhere and while it might not make much financial sense to live in your own property (it tends to work out to cost about $10,000 more per year), being on the property ladder is definitely needed in one shape or another to ensure financial security after retirement.

Other options

The problem with putting money in the bank is that you are unlikely to get an 8 per cent return. This means that you need to understand what other things you can put your money into, and how to grow your money faster. Investment options include:

- shares/stocks
- mutual funds
- property (commercial or residential)
- businesses
- term deposits
- KiwiSaver.

The average Kiwi does not have much money invested in shares. They might have been persuaded to buy shares in, say, Burger Fuel or Mighty River Power, but this is more due to a marketing push than them actually understanding the mechanics of what makes a good investment.

Shares

When I spoke to Sam Howard of First NZ Capital, he explained that shares are not typically used to grow wealth by teenagers or young adults, unless they have wealth to start with (usually by inheritance). There are a few reasons for this, but at its most basic, a child cannot enter into a financial contract. When you buy shares through a brokerage, you are entering a contract. You can circumvent this requirement by having someone over the age of 18 (normally a parent or grandparent) own the shares in trust for the child, although this often results in the investment being taxed at the parents' tax rate, which is usually a higher marginal rate. Further, if the investment is held in trust for the child, not only might a higher rate apply, but further administrative costs could be incurred through this ownership structure.

After the Global Financial Crisis of 2007–08, a lot of regulatory change came in, which means that the advice given by financial advisors is supposed to become more personalised. But for small investments (say under $250,000), the advice is execution or 'class' based, which is general in nature, which puts the onus back on the client. This is a bit of a pain, because if you have a 16-year-old who is keen on the market and just starting out without too much money, they aren't going to get the detailed advice they need because there isn't enough money tied into the investment (in the form of brokerage fees) to justify the financial advisor spending more time with them. For the above reasons, shares are not usually the first choice for growing small amounts of wealth for young people.

So what is a share, anyway? Let's peel this back to the basics. When a company wants to raise money so that they can expand and grow, they have the option of borrowing the money (from a bank or finance company), or to sell some shares in their company for a specific sum of money. This is called 'going public'—that is, the public can buy a share in that company. Shares are also known as stocks.

When you buy shares in a company, you own a tiny piece of that company. That is why a share or stock can also be called an equity. If the company does well, the value of the shares will rise; if the company does not do well, the share price will go down.

The shares of a company that has gone public are traded on a stock exchange. A stock exchange is just that: a place where you buy and sell stocks or shares. To buy and sell a stock you usually need to do it through a sharebroker and be over 18 years of age, with the minimum investment usually $500. Brokers are paid for each trade, with prices based on how much help and extra services they provide. A fee is deducted when you purchase a share (say 1 per cent), for the broker to manage your portfolio (a further 1 per cent) and to sell your shares. It is possible to buy some shares direct via the Smartshares system, which reduces the cost of acquisition to 0.5 per cent, but whichever way you cut it, someone is clipping the ticket.

Once you sign with a broker you are given an investor registration number that becomes the platform for buying or selling stock. Our market, the New Zealand Stock Exchange, is called the NZX for short, and it is open each business day from 10am to 5pm.

Shares are a great way to expose your kids to the wider world and help them learn to read and interpret financial statements. This is a skill that business owners need to master. Specifically, you want to be able to identify the total income earned, what the company spends on marketing, what the net profit is, what percentage of the profits are paid as a dividend, and how the company proposes to grow in the future. You are trying to break down the jargon and start to give your child confidence to understand the market and how to invest in it.

Mutual funds

A basic rule of investing is that you never want all your money to be invested in just one or two stocks. This is because if the stock goes down, you are going to be in trouble. Studies have shown that people are more nervous of downward movement than they are excited about upward movement. It's called loss aversion and can increase market volatility. They say that you need to be able to 'ride out' fluctuations in the market to be sure you will achieve long-term gains, but in reality, when the ship is sinking, few people are happy to 'ride it out', instead wanting to withdraw their funds while there are still funds to withdraw. We get nervous and the logic of waiting, selling or buying wisely often goes out the window.

The market affects the value of stock, and the value of stock influences the market—it is circular. There is an assumption that the players in the market are both informed and rational. But this assumption is false, often with media and uninformed people (often one and the same) making comments or tweets that can affect a company's value.

A stock mutual fund is simply a fund that owns dozens, if not hundreds, of individual stocks. It gives you instant diversification. You buy shares in a mutual fund, then each share gives you a stake in all the different stocks owned by that fund.

Another difference between owning shares and a mutual fund is that with shares you decide when to buy and sell. With a mutual fund, the fund manager decides when to buy or sell. You decide when you want to buy shares in the mutual fund, but the manager decides what is owned by the fund at any one time.

Much like shares, mutual funds need to be owned by an adult while your child is under the age of 18, which can make it harder for your child to be motivated to gain real insights into its operations as it is still removed from their reality. The best investment (in my view) to engage your kids is KiwiSaver.

KiwiSaver

KiwiSaver is a work-based, voluntary savings scheme set up by the government in July 2007. You can make voluntary contributions towards the fund and most importantly set one up in the name of your child, long before they start working. Funds cannot be easily withdrawn, so the most vital ingredient of compound interest, time, is allowed to work to create some solid results.

If you set up a fund before your child is 15, it is likely that you will have at least 10 years before they might need the funds for a possible first-home purchase. This means you can choose to invest in a growth or aggressive type of fund for a longer period of time, so the return is likely to be higher. If you start early enough, it will provide a nice amount to assist your child with their first home.

The reason why KiwiSaver works so well is the time element. It is easy for textbooks to say that the market will go up and down, but you need to stay in for the long haul to be sure to get the benefits. In reality, though, if the world economy is tanking, and if you have the option to withdraw funds, most of us would take advantage of this, even though we know that withdrawing funds at the wrong time is the way you realise the loss.

KiwiSaver removes our ability to access funds, ironically giving the fund a better chance to succeed over time, because it has the time it needs. Not only does KiwiSaver give higher returns than money in the bank (provided you are in the right type of fund), it can also overcome the quandary of who owns what, as the KiwiSaver fund can be opened in the name of the child and taxed at the child's rate. When the child starts working part time (hopefully from the age of 15), their contribution plus the government's plus their employer's is all pooled together to

COMPOUND INTEREST IN ACTION WITH KIWISAVER

If you invested $1500 per annum into a KiwiSaver fund for your child, for the first 18 years of their life, you would deposit $27,000 over this timeframe. At an 8 per cent return, this fund would increase to $56,175, with $29,175 (more than half of the funds) coming from compound interest. This investment will be subject to inflation in the sense that $56,175 in 18 years' time will buy less than it does today. Adjusting for inflation ($12,332), you would still have $43,843.

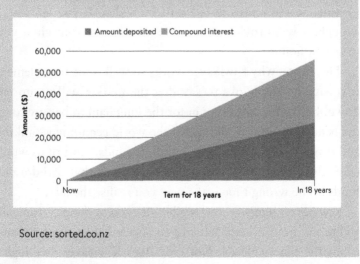

Source: sorted.co.nz

help grow the base investment faster. Grandparents can also make contributions when they want.

The downside with KiwiSaver is that funds can only be withdrawn to purchase a first home or on retirement. This isn't particularly helpful to your child if they are wanting to pay for their tertiary studies or OE. Personally, I think this lack of accessibility is an advantage. Certainly, the government could change the first-home-buyer rules, but this seems unlikely in my view, and even if they did make it harder to access funds for a first home, the investment will continue to grow and the rewards are yours for retirement or in financial hardship.

Property

Property is a key investment class for most Kiwis, although it is not as passive as other investment options. We get it: we can touch it, borrow against it (leverage it), insure it, improve it and usually see it go up in value over time. If it is an investment, there are likely to be tax benefits, and it can be easily owned by a syndicate.

The property market does not move in a straight, upward line, and the gains we are currently experiencing are unlikely to be sustained in the long term. Instead the market moves in cycles. At the start of the cycle, interest rates can be high and credit is tight. Towards the end of the cycle, credit frees up, interest rates are lowered and it's easier to get loans. At some points in the cycle, property can stop going up in value and even drop. This is a problem if you are forced to sell the property at this point. Your goal is to have a strong enough financial situation to be able to ride out the downward fluctuations in the property market.

Not all properties are created equal, and not all of them will increase in value over time. In my view, you only want to invest in property if the long-term return justifies it. You want to make sure the property is likely to go up in value. Key drivers of property prices are:
- population growth
- interest rates

- new housing consents
- global factors
- rental growth
- affordability
- property type.

The type of property purchased can have as much bearing on the capital gain as the location. Property types include: apartment, townhouse unit, standalone, cross-leased, and freehold.

Remember, the gains are not linear, the property market goes up and down, and sometimes it even stays still. You need to be able to hold the property through the bad times in order to realise its capital-gain potential. This makes sense, but a lot of people will get burnt from a correction in the cycle. If interest rates increase more than 2 per cent (back to where they were just a couple of years ago), there will be a lot of hurt, which will play out in houses being sold at a discount—less than what they were purchased for, and possibly less than the amount of debt owing. If you are on the receiving end of this, you will be in for a world of pain.

In determining what drives property values, you need to understand the basic economic notion of supply and demand. If there is a limited supply, or high demand, then prices increase. If there is excess supply or low demand, then prices drop. Simple. But what drives this?

Demand is ultimately driven by the number of people who need a house to live in. This is driven by net migration, internal migration (between cities) and organic population growth. Net migration is the difference between the number of people coming into New Zealand and the number leaving. We are currently experiencing some of the highest net migration in New

Zealand's history. It is not sustainable at this level, although there are probably a few more years left in this run.

In conjunction with net migration, you also have organic population growth, which takes into account births, deaths and increasing life spans. When considering what areas to invest in, not all locations are created equal. Just because the population is increasing doesn't mean the value of properties in your town will increase. People move to where there is work.

Statistics New Zealand prepares calculations on the projected population growth of different council areas beyond 2031, which is helpful in narrowing down your investment options. But this is only the tip of what needs to be considered when determining what property is going to work for you and your family in the long run. Attention needs to be paid to the suburb itself in which you are investing and the type of property, in addition to interest rates, tax benefits and the overall financial top-up you will need to meet expenses. For more details on this, read my book *Kill Your Mortgage and Sort Your Retirement*.

Commercial property

Much like residential property, commercial property allows you to leverage by borrowing up to 65 per cent of the property's value from the bank. The rent received relative to the purchase price is higher than with residential property, while the holding costs are lower (as the tenant covers the rates, etc.). The disadvantage is that interest rates tend to be higher and vacancy periods longer. The higher price and larger deposit required than a typical residential rental can also be a barrier to entry, but if you can get into the commercial market it can be a good place to be.

TERM DEPOSITS

A term deposit is a cash investment placed with a financial institution (usually a bank) for an agreed period, known as the 'term'. Interest is earned and paid at the end of the term. Term deposits are not usually an effective way of growing your wealth, as the interest rate may be on par with or slightly higher than the inflation rate, but they are considered one of the safest forms of investment and an option for people who have no tolerance for risk.

BUSINESSES

Wealth creation through business is one of my favourite strategies for growth, although not everyone does this successfully and the failure rate can be high (especially within the first couple of years after commencement). What I love about business as a means of growing your wealth is if you are willing to put in some effort, and that's coupled with a well-run business and ripe market conditions, it can translate to a great return. Some people want to run a business because it can give them a certain lifestyle and it allows them to dictate how much they earn, but I don't really buy into this philosophy. The truth is that, if you run a business well, you will be working harder than you would have as an employee, and the cash flow constraints of the business will often dictate how much you can actually be paid—but a well-run business can also be an effective way of creating value and increased earnings. It doesn't take a university education to run a business, nor does it always require much capital to get started. Although the latter can help.

LEVERAGE

As a parent, when you have leverage against your child, you have the power. We know leverage to be a beautiful thing, in that it gives you more power than usual to get what you want.

Financially speaking, leverage is when you use people's money, time and energy for your own advancement. In business, you leverage off your staff to increase sales, or as a landlord, you leverage off your tenant to pay your mortgage. But the classic version of leverage is when you leverage off the bank: when you use some of your own money or equity to create a deposit for a property, then use the bank's money to complete the purchase. The beauty of leverage is that you only put in say 20 per cent of the value, but keep 100 per cent of the gain.

Mastering leverage with property is what is going to allow your kids to get on to the property ladder (albeit at a low rung) quickly, then allow them to systematically move up. The concept of leverage, and the unfair advantage it provides, is what can set property apart from other investments.

Leverage is using debt to grow your wealth faster. It comes with risks, as not all properties are created equal. Not all properties will increase in value, and certainly not at the same rate. But if you can start to understand these obstacles, then learn to work around them, property, in conjunction with leverage, can be your friend.

Let me illustrate leverage working for you. Let's say you are buying an investment property for $350,000. In the three scenarios below you have different levels of deposit, meaning the amount of money you borrow from the bank varies.

Purchase price	Deposit	Leverage	Bank borrowing
$350,000	$350,000	nil	nil
$350,000	$175,000	50%	$175,000
$350,000	$70,000	80%	$280,000

Putting the type of property and the corresponding top-up to one side, let's assume the property goes up in value 6 per cent every year. In the space of 10 years the property will be worth around $600,000, irrespective of the level of money you invested initially or the level of debt you had to take on to facilitate the purchase.

All three scenarios mean that you have made $250,000 as a minimum, being the difference between the current value and the purchase price. If you purchased the property outright with no funding, that gives you a return on your investment of 79 per cent over the 10 years, which is pretty good.

But if you decided to borrow 50 per cent of the purchase price from the bank, using $175,000 of your own money and borrowing the rest, this would mean your initial equity in the property would have been lower as the bank would have owned $175,000 or half of its value. But the bank's ownership is limited to the funds borrowed, so the return on your investment is actually higher, at 158 per cent, and you have gone from owning 50 per cent of the property to 71 per cent of the property over 10 years without paying down debt.

What's more, if you had only used a 20 per cent deposit, borrowing 80 per cent of the purchase price, you would only have to had put $70,000 of your own equity upfront, which when coupled with the leverage would have given you a 395 per cent return on your initial investment. You go from owning 20 per cent of the property initially to 53 per cent of the property because of the capital gain. The return on investment is magnified over time, so within say 17 years you would own 73 per cent of the property. This is without paying down any of the mortgage, and assumes rent covers the outgoings.

Another, more discreet, benefit of debt over time is that with the benefit of inflation the value of the debt is lower. The higher the rate of inflation, the less your debt is worth year on year. In the KiwiSaver example, without inflation your investment would be worth $57,000 in 18 years' time, but with inflation this would reduce to $43,000, because each dollar will have less buying power in 18 years' time. So inflation counts against cash investments, because each year they need to increase by the rate of inflation to be worth the same amount or have the same value 12 months later. With debt, inflation is your friend, because each year your debt is worth less.

Let me illustrate: since 2000, CPI (Consumers Price Index) inflation has averaged 2.7 per cent, so if you had an investment of $100,000 back then, it would need to have increased to $143,000 today to buy the same amount of goods. This is because of inflation, which is referred to as the 'thief in your pocket'. It eats away at the hard work of compound interest. This means you need to make sure your investment's return is higher than inflation, otherwise you are going nowhere.

But if you have debt, inflation isn't a thief, it's your financial angel. For example, if you had $100,000 of debt in 2000 and didn't repay it for 17 years (presuming you didn't have to pay any interest), you would still owe $100,000. To owe the same value of debt your debt would have had to increase to $143,000, but it hasn't. This is a real gain to you of $30,000, because $100,000 in 2017 is the equivalent of $70,000 of debt that has increased at the rate of inflation over the following 17 years.

As a parent, you don't need to be an expert on wealth-creation strategies, but you do need to know enough about what life costs and whether or not your child's chosen career path is going to allow them to be financially successful. In most instances, it won't, even if they have taken the right or best career path. Your job is to widen your child's eyes to the less-traditional ways of earning money and creating wealth, helping them grasp the concept of leverage and when it pays to utilise it. Introduce them to a financial advisor or successful entrepreneur if you need to, but don't leave them to fumble financially through their early adulthood. They may be still 'finding themselves', but no matter what they find or when exactly they find it, they will still need to be well versed in wealth-creation strategies.

HOW THE BANKING SYSTEM WORKS

We give our money to the bank to keep it safe, and the bank turns around and gives it to someone else to make the money they need to pay you and still make a profit. They are required to keep some of the money you deposit with them on hand, as capital, but can lend out the rest. But they also leverage against the deposits, lending out more than they have, creating money as part of this process, although this is kept in check by the Reserve Bank, which stipulates the level of capital reserves that the banks must keep on hand.

Traditional economic books would tell you that if you deposit $100 at a bank, it might keep $10 back as liquid funds, then lend out $90 of the money received into the economy for someone else to be able to buy a house or a car, money which is eventually deposited at another bank, which then on-lends $81 of this. Of the money in the economy only 3 per cent is physical cash and the rest is in electronic deposits or electronic loans. However, in New Zealand, for every $100 you deposit at the bank, the bank is able to on-lend $150 (not $90), creating $50 of deposits that doesn't physically exist. And we wonder why it turns bad, when the banks are actually creating money that doesn't exist!

GOOD AND BAD DEBT

Debt is owing anything to anyone for any reason. To have incurred debt, you have spent money before you have earned it. It includes money owed on credit cards, car loans, finance cards, mortgages and student loans. Some of these debts may have been incurred for a good reason, but this doesn't mean they are 'good debt'.

Our kids are growing up in the most indebted generation in history. The average university graduate leaves with $20,000–$50,000 of debt and this increases yearly. The annual cost of studying can be as much as $20,000 if you are living away from home, sometimes higher.

The problem with debt is that it makes people look better than they really are. Debt can allow you to look like someone that you aren't, and as if you are doing better than you are.

Our culture is confused about debt. Some debt is better than other debt. Some debt is bad and some is neither good nor bad. Understanding this concept is key for wealth creation and financial-disaster avoidance. Borrowing money to invest in an asset that increases in value can be a good investment.

Good debt is money you borrow for something that is going to make you money, save you money, or increase in value at a rate higher than the cost of the debt. Property is the most common example of this. A student loan could be another example of good debt, as you are borrowing money to invest in yourself, to allow you to make more money than you would otherwise have made. But it is only a good investment if it allows you to grow your income at a faster long-term rate than not having a loan.

A lot of studies suggest that university graduates make more money than people who don't attend university, but when you factor in the cash repayment (12 cents has to be repaid to the government for every $1 earned), and the fact that it has taken you three or four years of little or no income to get to that point, the initial cash flow benefits might not be as obvious as the original claim suggests.

Bad debt is money you borrow for something that won't go up in value at the same rate as the interest incurred to purchase the item, or more commonly is for an item that decreases in value like cars, holidays, furniture and other consumer items. You can't always avoid bad debt, but the amount and how much it costs you can be minimised.

If your child does get into debt, avoid trying to bail them out. Show them how they need to fix the problem and what behaviours are needed to change their financial landscape, or pay for them to have some financial coaching.

As an exercise with your kids, list all your debts (in broad terms). Explain to them which are good and which are bad. (However, if you only have bad debt, you are kind of undermining the lesson—so get it sorted out.)

Teach your children that if you owe money and you have money, it makes sense to pay the money owed with the money you have, especially if the interest rate on the owed money is higher than the interest rate you are earning on your held money. If you have savings, use them to pay off your credit card (provided you still have enough money left as an emergency fund and that the interest rate is higher on the credit card than the savings rates).

Very simply, if you are borrowing to buy an asset that goes up in value, and it is increasing in value more than the borrowed funds are costing you, then this is good debt or productive debt. If you are borrowing to buy something that goes down in value—then this debt is bad and dumb.

BUILDING A CREDIT RATING

There is an argument that you need to incur debt to build a strong credit rating. The algorithm used to determine your credit rating involves a few different items, which US author Dave Ramsey breaks down:

- 35 per cent is based on your debt-payment history
- 30 per cent on your debt levels
- 15 per cent on the length of debt
- 10 per cent on new debt, and
- 10 per cent on the type of debt.

So that means 100 per cent of the score is based on debt, not wealth. In determining your credit score, no consideration is made of your wealth, income or retirement savings. It is not based on you paying for everything in cash.

Your credit score has no bearing on how successful you are with money; it simply indicates how good you are at borrowing money.

A credit score is a number between 0 and 1000 that indicates how credit-worthy you are, and how likely you are to pay your bills on time. Most people's credit scores are between 300 and 850, according to Credit Simple, a leading credit bureau in New

Zealand. A good score is more than 500. In other countries, a good credit score usually means you can get lower interest rates with banks and other lending institutions, but I am yet to see that in New Zealand; here, banks are more concerned with whether you have a bad credit rating (that is, whether you owe money to anyone, have been bankrupt, or if you have unpaid fines) than whether your credit score is good. This is because having a good credit score in isolation doesn't show the level of equity you have, or how much money you earn or save. Employers and landlords are starting to enquire about prospective employees' or tenants' credit scores, much like requiring new employees to participate in voluntary drug tests.

If you have never applied for credit, you probably won't have a credit score. This means those under the age of 18, as people are not likely to have a credit card, utility account or similar until after they leave home.

Credit cards

Credit cards should be used for emergencies only and should be paid off when you use them, not at the end of the month. Being able to pay your credit card bill in full each month tells you that you are breaking even. Yet culturally it is seen as some measure of success. It isn't. I actually don't care about the number of points you make on your credit card, if you are making no progress overall. It is a false economy.

The problem I have with paying off a credit card at the end of each month is that you are doing everything in reverse. You are not driving to a destination; you are paying for things you have already done with money you haven't earned. You would be considered a lousy businessman if you did this, and you are lousy with your personal finances if you continue this belief. It's like driving a car by looking in the rear-view mirror. You can only see where you have been, you don't know where you are going and what you need to do to get you there.

By the time your kids are leaving school they will be getting bombarded with credit-card offers and overdraft facilities. Both are good for emergencies, but if they become part of day-to-day living, they will financially weaken your child.

You need your kids to understand that real money—cash—carries more emotional weight than plastic. The danger of plastic not having the same weight as real money is that people spend more when using plastic than cash, sometimes up to 30 per cent more.

I have had one client say that they have given their child a credit card to help teach them responsibility. I was like, 'Are you kidding me?' Credit cards don't teach responsibility. They teach you that you can buy something you can't afford today, and you can worry about paying for it later. The pain of the purchase is not connected to the receipt of goods. If you are teaching them that credit cards are OK, you are putting a 10-year delay on their financial journey.

Borrowing to buy a car

Too many people incur debt to buy a car they can't afford. This is classic 'big hat no cattle' culture.

What do you do? You sell the car. You will never get out of debt or build wealth if you have a car payment that is sucking out 20 per cent of your income.

If you do need to borrow to buy a car, then you buy the cheapest car you can find. If you can't repay the car loan in under three years, while still making financial progress elsewhere, then you have borrowed more than you can afford and that whole champagne taste on a beer budget will be the main driver of your lack of progress.

SUPPORTING YOUR KIDS

How do you support your kids in their dreams when you know they are not likely to become a reality?

The value of education is not that it equips you for a specific job, but it can prepare you for multiple career options. A great education equips you for a full life, not just a job.

If you do encourage your kids to follow their dreams, you better make sure they are aware of the financial implications of this decision. They need to know what they are likely to earn and what they will need in terms of qualifications. Help them make as informed a decision as possible. There also has to be a plan B, especially if you are going to be supporting them in some way while they are studying.

And before they know what they will study or do as a career, they will need to know more about themselves.

Career advice

Parenting is not necessarily about shaping a child, but unwrapping a child, which becomes obvious when they are trying to determine what career path they want to go down. In choosing a path they need to understand what they like, what they are good at, what soft skills they have (see later in this chapter), how confident they are and whether they work well in groups. To help with this, your child might do some personality or aptitude tests to get a general sense of where they might be headed. In addition to this, they need to have an understanding of the type of lifestyle they want to be able to live, to determine whether the career path they want to go down can provide this, or if they need to adjust their lifestyle expectations.

The New Zealand labour market is highly dynamic. Around 200,000 jobs are created every year and 150,000 are disestablished. The average person will work for 12 different organisations and have four different careers during their working lifetime. We need to master skills that can transition us to various jobs.

Remind your child that it is not chance, but choice, that determines a financial future. You need to show them the reality of their career choices, or at the very least introduce them to someone who can. I know that some schools have career evenings, but these happen too late in kids' schooling and the jobs illustrated often do not even touch the iceberg of possible career paths.

In addition to their possible career path, kids need to understand that structure + framework = freedom (or choice), and that income can be earned as a salary or profit, and from working for someone or working for yourself.

In trying to ascertain a career, kids are likely to call on the career advisors at their school, although not all schools have one. In my research for this book I met with different career advisors, all passionate about helping kids understand their options after school, but all equally open about how the lack of time available (on average 30 minutes every year or two per child) makes it hard to be truly effective in their role.

I tried to familiarise myself with the process the career advisor might go through in the limited time they did have. It was commonplace to work with the child to do some basic rudimentary personality test like Myers-Briggs, which is supposed to provide an indication of the strengths of their personality type and align them with careers that might work—

if they can understand the questions being asked by the test. When I tried to complete it, I struggled with what the questions were asking, and I am not sure if I would have understood it or have had significant enough life experience to respond to it at the age of 16 or 17.

If answered correctly it can help illuminate the communication and learning styles of your personality. When I completed the test I found some of the findings were spot on, while others were incorrect. It does not promise to be accurate, nor is it gospel. For me, it did not help identify any skills or suitable career choices (in my mind), but it is a starting point for discussion, and when you are dealing with 16- or 17-year-olds you always need a place to start! Essentially, you need time to be able to interpret and work though the assessment to understand the results more fully, and that time just isn't available to school career advisors.

The government's careers.govt.nz website gives salary indications, which is a helpful starting place, but this needs to be accompanied by an understanding of what your lifestyle could cost, along with your skill set and personality strengths, to have any real meaning. The website nomajordrama.co.nz has information about university majors, selecting from all the majors available which one is best suited to the applicant.

I went to the website to see what majors I should have done based on what I know about myself now. The site asks a few questions, sometimes more than once. It felt like a trip to the optometrist where you are not sure if they are showing you a new image or the old image over again! It is helpful to a point, but the career suggested was so far from what I like that I can only assume I misunderstood a question.

While these are definitely helpful tools, you have to have a career in mind for this to help. Personally, I am not convinced a

17-year-old would answer some questions accurately and could risk going off on a tangent career by mistake if relying on these websites in isolation. I believe what is needed is to be able to discuss the reality of different careers with different people in different fields, one on one, to understand the different jobs that emerge from various degrees and what each job entails on a day-to-day basis.

In speaking with the advisors, it was clear that there remains a push for kids to go to university, although there has recently been a move to promote the trades again. Some kids are opting for this route over university, which is great, especially if they were never going to get out of university what they needed.

I was curious as to how the advisors handled kids who have crazy notions about what they want to do, as this is more common than we might think. Kids are being taught to only do something that they are 'passionate' about. How passionate can a 17-year-old be about something, when their frame of reference is so narrow, one might ask? Where they can, the advisors try to encourage a plan B, or at least some consideration about whether a business can be built around the idea. But they feel their hands are tied and they don't have enough time to be a real influencer of change.

Anecdotally, it seems all advisors believe the kids could benefit from more financial education that covers off tax, repaying student loans, how much you will earn and what type of lifestyle this will give you. This would certainly help—along with universities not telling impressionable kids that you need to have two degrees to 'get a look in', and teachers telling kids that the job market is changing significantly, and that there are jobs today that won't exist in 10 years, and jobs that have not yet been invented. If they are going to say these sorts of things, then they need to underpin their comments with the idea that change creates opportunity and there are some laws of nature that apply irrespective of change, otherwise it is plain scaremongering.

Our kids will need to be able to work collaboratively, adapt quickly and have a strong emotional intelligence. Despite all this change, there are still things that underpin society that won't change. People will buy what makes them happy, and will always try and keep up with the Joneses. Supply and demand underpin the price of goods. Idiots will always be able to vote. War drives innovation; time and chance happens to everyone. You reap what you sow, even if you are a good talker. Most great learning comes in groups. Having children usually grounds you.

Why is there such a push towards university?

I asked some advisors why there is such a push towards university when kids don't even know what they want to do, and when the cost is so high to attend, and when one in two university graduates in the US are working in jobs that do not require the degree they attained. There was no adequate answer, although there was a general sense of 'they need to go somewhere and university is better than doing nothing'. Which of course is true . . . unless they do nothing at university, in which case they were better off staying at home and saving themselves $50,000.

Many professions stipulate certain tertiary qualifications as a minimum requirement. So if getting a degree is going to link you to your chosen profession, then it is a good investment. For example, one friend of mine studied medicine. She has a $100,000 student loan, but she has found her vocation and is chomping away at her loan. Another friend also completed a medical degree, also has $100,000 of debt, and has now decided she wants to be a teacher.

If the debt incurred to achieve a qualification dictates a higher entitlement to income, we call this 'good debt'. But not all university debt is good debt—not if you end up working in a job that does not require the degree you have achieved and incurred a student loan to do so. That is not good debt. For those people, I would say university could have been an expensive waste of time. If it didn't cost too much it wouldn't be so much of an issue, because the thing school-leavers seem to have in spades is time. But if the university does cost—and in cases where you need to leave home to study, then it costs a lot—then you need to have a better idea of where you are going, surely.

Making an informed choice

You want your kid to make an informed choice, whatever they decide. You don't want them to go to university for the sake of it. However, if they find their calling while they're there, I guess it's worth it.

The problem I found, when I interviewed Year 12 and 13 students, is that a lot are motivated by TV, which glamorises the most boring of roles. Most wanted to be lawyers (thanks to Harvey and Mike from *Suits*). Some had researched the income these roles paid, but few had looked into the number of positions that are available to entry-level graduates, and only one had worked in a law firm (that his dad owned).

It's OK for kids not to go to university straight after school. Having a gap year can be great. I had one client who decided to become a hairdresser. She dropped out of school after sixth form (Year 12) and started out on $20,000 per year. Now she runs a salon and makes more than $150,000 per year. She earns more money than most of my university-graduate clients. Just saying.

The purpose of university is to open your eyes to the world, and to help you to become more employable. But it only satisfies one of the key things that any future employer is looking for. They want to know that you can learn—yes. University and school can demonstrate this. But they also want to know that you have emotional intelligence and are adaptable, and university does not teach you this.

What are employers looking for?

I heard from a group of students that a university dean had presented at their school and told them that in order to distinguish themselves from their peers they now needed to do two degrees. I was surprised to hear that, but because it's been 15 years since I graduated, I wondered if I was out of touch with the new norm. I decided to speak with various HR directors, managers and recruiters to get a better sense of what employers are looking for today. And guess what: it wasn't two degrees. Certainly, two degrees could help if they are directly relevant to the role, otherwise one degree was perfectly adequate. Pretty much everyone recognises that having a degree is only the start of the journey.

For the most part, employers are looking for 'soft skills'. These are seen as transferrable skills as the technical components of any role can be learned, but soft skills less so.

Soft skills are a combination of interpersonal and social skills, including communication skills, character traits, attitudes and emotional intelligence (EQ), which enable people to effectively operate in their social environment, work well with others and perform well in the workplace. Soft skills do not require academic knowledge, but require awareness, and can be improved.

Employers see a university degree as proof of ability to learn, and a base competence in a particular discipline. Beyond that, on-the-job training and exposure to the different types of roles and specific skills needed are more important.

Unlike technical skills that can be measured from educational background and work experience, soft skills are a major differentiator for employability and success in life. A study conducted by Harvard University noted that 80 per cent of a person's achievements in their career are determined by soft skills, and only 20 per cent by 'hard' skills specific to that industry or position. A study conducted by McDonald's in the UK predicted that over half a million people will be held back from various job sectors by 2020 due to a lack of soft skills.

EQ (emotional intelligence) and AQ (adaptable intelligence) are now surpassing IQ. Employers are just as interested in a graduate's willingness to learn and whether they have good communication skills, humility and curiosity. A red flag to an employer would be someone who is overly ideological or unable to articulate answers or communicate well. Working while at school or university helps develop the skills future employers are trying to harness.

Emotional and adaptable intelligence

To succeed in the future, our kids need to be better and smarter than previous generations. They need to be able to adapt themselves. The room for making dumb decisions is narrower than before, because the physical cost and opportunity cost of these decisions will put them on a course of financial inadequacy and parental dependency for longer than is sustainable.

Our kids need to learn to seek broader perspectives (which is ironic, given the filter of social media usually personifies a narrow view as you tend to follow who you like and create your own ecosystem of shallowness). They don't need to be child prodigies to succeed. In fact, the link between child prodigy and adult genius is weak, according to psychologist Ellen Winner—perhaps because to be a child prodigy you need to be able to learn, and to be a successful adult, you need to be a masterful doer, which are two different concepts entirely. Child prodigies are always the teacher's pets, yet to paraphrase T.S. Eliot, their careers tend to end not with a bang, but a whimper. The gifted are not socially awkward but fail to be original. Practice makes perfect, but it doesn't make new. They lack creativity. Interestingly, the most creative children are least likely to don the title of 'favourite' growing up.

EQ is what turns intention into action, to be able to overcome challenges, defuse conflict and communicate effectively. It is learned, and the learning starts young. EQ is defined as a combination of self-awareness, self-management, social awareness and relationship management. All helicopter parenting has a detrimental effect on this. EQ must be cultivated by parents giving room to our kids to learn, try, practise, fail and press forward within the safety of home base.

Adaptable intelligence, also described as fluid intelligence, on the other hand, has to do with the ability to be adaptable and solve problems, to think on your feet, think outside the box and come up with creative approaches to new situations, to improvise even in an unfamiliar situation. If you hear people talk about 'street smarts', they are more or less describing fluid intelligence. Fluid intelligence gets its name from the non-linear nature of these thought processes, which are ever-changing, just as the nature of fluid is always changing to adapt to the shape of its container. Fluid intelligence requires a sense of awareness and open-mindedness, neither of which are necessarily required of IQ.

Because jobs are being created and being made redundant

at a fast rate of knots, focus needs to be spent on being able to demonstrate you can learn (IQ), but also develop EQ and AQ. Technology will replace some basic jobs, but it will always be limited to non-creative aspects of the workforce. Creative thinking will be what sets adults apart from each other, and financial progress will come down to those who are able to think differently about how they work and create wealth.

The tools that we use and that our parents used will not work for our kids. They need to think creatively about their finances, be able to work on a strategy for financial success and move forward faster. The great thing is that money is one of the strongest motivators for learning.

THE OPTION OF SELF-EMPLOYMENT

Most of us start as an employee and then, if we want to become self-employed, we transition to it. Being self-employed gives you more freedom, but also comes with more responsibility. Most claim the reason for becoming self-employed is that they want to be their own boss, have more certainty, to be in control of their own destiny, work their own hours, earn more money, and grow and develop a concept.

When I interviewed school-leavers, many expressed a desire to be their own boss because they believed they would be safer and more secure if they create their own jobs rather than depending on the uncertainties of the economy. There was also a romanticism around them being able to do something meaningful, which of course leads to them changing the world (in their own eyes, at least).

The reasons for becoming self-employed are valid. In practice, not everyone achieves them. In reality, when you are your own boss it is easy to work just as many hours, if not more than when you were an employee. The income may be better, but costs need to be deducted from that and tax paid. The compliance aspects of being your own boss can be a killer, especially if you do not excel at admin.

As the business grows, of course you can outsource the components of the business that you don't like doing, but you have to grow the business first. To grow a business without the wheels falling off is tricky. People say you have to work 'on' the business, not in it, but the reality is that when you are small, you do not have the luxury of taking your foot off the accelerator while you look under the hood. You are on the tools to make money, to pay the bills, to make the treadmill keep moving. Working on the business is done after hours when you should be sleeping. This is the reality for many.

But if you do it right, being self-employed can be the best thing that ever happened to you. It can be an opportunity to earn more money, but this is not guaranteed. Like most things, you have to be able to leverage your time and other people's time if you are going to make a good crack of it.

The discussion you need to have with your child is that they needn't become an employee for the rest of their life, especially if all their personality traits suggest they need to be their own boss. If they have identified a likelihood of this happening, they need to position themselves for the maximum chance of success. This means that they need to learn from someone experienced in the field they want to go into.

They will likely need to be employed to do this, with the sole purpose of learning the practicalities of the job, on the job; to gather knowledge that they can put to use for their own benefit at a later point. The smartest way to learn is through other people's mistakes or experiences. Your child needn't know the particular business they will operate in, or the business idea itself. But they should start to glean an idea of the industry they want to work in, knowing that from there a business idea or opportunity will come.

Remind your kids that no matter how amazing the business idea they have is, for the business to have legs, they need to be able to make money from it. They will need to find a way to sustain themselves, and the business idea. Working backwards from what their life will cost will give you the minimum profit the business will need to pay out in order for the idea to be profitable.

New Zealand has one of the highest levels of self-employment in the world and is considered one of the easiest places in the world to start your own business. Self-employment numbers are expected to increase further in coming years as more employers make permanent positions redundant, preferring freelancers or contractors to cover positions previously held by employees. This means more of our kids will be their own boss earlier (whether they want to or not). They will need to learn how to spend their time efficiently and understand how to set goals, prioritise tasks and make choices around what ideas or projects to pursue.

To be your own boss, you need to understand business. To understand business, you need to be comfortable with the numbers that underpin the overall results of the business. Once you understand the numbers, you connect the drivers or inputs that will affect the results so you can focus on certain actions to help change an outcome. Kids will need to know how businesses work to be comfortable in this space. Personally, I think all students should be required to study business at school. It is as important as maths and English if not more so.

When they transition to the real world, especially if they plan on being an entrepreneur, they will need to be able to make a case for themselves. The argument they will need to present to potential backers is not 'I need money because it's a really good idea'. This might work when they are 10 years old, but shouldn't cut the mustard after that. Your kids have to think along the lines of 'I need X dollars that will result in X result, and in X time. I can provide you with X return on your investment, or save you X.' We are talking real-world stuff here, not the imaginary world we immerse our kids in when they should be transitioning to adulthood. Most of the young adults I work with need coaching in this area, and parents aren't usually the ones to do it effectively.

Insights into being an entrepreneur

When I interviewed millennials, more than half had a romantic view of the world. They wanted to make an impact (whatever that means). If they were going to start a business, they wanted to put all their energy into it, and not focus on working a day job so they had more time and commitment to invest in their business idea. This is kind of cool—but usually comes at a cost to their parents, not themselves. They see themselves taking a risk and backing themselves, which they reminded me is the essence of an entrepreneur.

To counter this, I looked into a management study referenced in Adam Grant's book *Originals: How Non-Conformists Move the World*. Researchers Joseph Raffiee and Jie Feng of the University of Wisconsin-Madison asked the simple question: when people start a business, are they better off keeping or quitting their day jobs (or, in the case of a millennials, actually getting a day job, to then quit). From 1994–2008 they tracked over 5000 people in their twenties, thirties, forties and fifties who became entrepreneurs.

The study showed that the ones who took the full plunge were risk-takers and had oodles of confidence. The remainder, who hedged their bets by continuing to work while starting their company, were far more risk-averse and less sure of themselves, taking greater measures to build the business to last.

Most would predict a clear advantage to the risk-taker. Yet the study showed the exact opposite. Entrepreneurs who kept their day jobs had 33 per cent lower odds of failure than those who quit their jobs.

The interesting thing about entrepreneurs is that they don't like risk any more than anyone else, but they are prepared to take calculated risks. As teenagers, successful entrepreneurs were nearly three times as likely as their peers to break rules.

SUCCESSFUL PROCRASTINATION

When you plan, plan strategically. If you procrastinate, procrastinate strategically.

At school and home, our kids are taught that acting early is the key to success, and when it comes to assignments at school, this is probably true. In business we're told that speed has its advantages and being first to the market pays. But in business many of the advantages of being first are easily balanced and at times outweighed by the disadvantages. In his book *Zero to One*, entrepreneur Peter Thiel writes 'Moving first is a tactic, not a goal. Being the first mover doesn't do you any good if someone else comes along and unseats you.'

Today, being late is seen as being disorganised or unproductive. But before we became fixated on productivity and efficiency, procrastination had two meanings: one, denoting laziness, and two, waiting for the right time.

Analysis completed by Bill Gross, the founder of Idealab, which has been involved with the start-up of over 100 companies, found what drove success. 'The number one thing is timing,' Gross revealed. Not uniqueness of idea, the capabilities of the team, the quality of the business model or funding, but timing accounted for 42 per cent of the difference between success and failure. One study of over 3000 start-ups indicates that roughly three out of every four fail because of premature scaling (growing too fast)—making investments the market isn't ready to support. Too many businesses fail because they are ahead of their time.

From a creative perspective, the positive spin on procrastination is sometimes referred to as the Zeigarnik effect. Bluma Zeigarnik was a Russian psychologist who demonstrated in 1927 that people have a better memory for incomplete or interrupted tasks than complete tasks. Once a task is finished, we stop thinking about it. When a task is interrupted and left uncompleted, it stays active in our minds. For example, completing an assignment early doesn't leave you open to new ideas and limits brainstorming.

Procrastination can keep us open to other ideas. If you procrastinate, procrastinate strategically. Make gradual progress by refining possibilities.

CONCLUSION

Creating wealth is less about how much money you earn and more about what you do with the money you have left over. This will be a relief for some kids and their parents, whose income levels are likely to be limited through their choice of career. Wealth creation starts with understanding how the banking system operates, and how you need to work that system to your benefit. In order to decide which wealth-creation option is going to be the best for getting you where you want to be by the time you want to be there, you need to understand the range of wealth-creation options that are available to you. The best way to do this is to first determine which options are not available to you, then focus on what you can work with and determine if you will need to leverage and how best to do so. The right strategy is the one that gets you where you need to be by working with what you have got.

The range of wealth-creation options is vast, from more passive options such as KiwiSaver to more active ones such as establishing and growing a business. Some people might only need one wealth-creation strategy to get them where they want to be; others will need multiple strategies, working concurrently. And, while of course what works for one person might not work for another, there are two very basic principles that your children need to understand: spend less than you earn, and understand how leverage functions in business and in the property market. Give your child the confidence to understand how the banking system works by talking about it with them, and by explaining the wealth-creation option (or options) you have applied yourself. Discuss the pitfalls and the opportunities created. Conversation builds confidence—or, at the very least, it demystifies the behind-the-scenes work that is done by those who seem to be jumping ahead financially, and helps your kids understand what additional steps are needed to complement their career choice and increase their odds of financial success.

CHAPTER 9
SPECIAL ISSUES FACING OUR GIRLS

As parents, we need all the help we can get to see that the most loving thing we can do for our kids is to not overindulge them. We need to share the truth about money and relationships so they steer themselves in the right direction. This is particularly relevant for our daughters, who will face more challenges than their male siblings.

WORKING PARENTS AND DIVORCE

Divorce is rarely discussed in connection with the shift of women from home to work. There is little doubt that the greater ability of women to support themselves and their children outside of marriage is an important factor in the post-1960s increase in divorce rates. In his book *The Great Risk Shift*, American author

Jacob S. Hacker points out that across the Western world, 'divorce has become more common precisely when and where women's participation in the labour force has expanded'.

The probability of a first marriage ending in divorce or separation within 10 years rose from 14 per cent in the 1950s to 30 per cent by the late 1980s. Compared with a generation ago, the ability of women to sustain themselves economically outside of marriage has certainly increased, yet the financial effects of divorce on families, and especially women, are frequently devastating.

We now live in a world where both parents need to be earning, so when only one parent is working and raising kids mostly or on their own, they face dire circumstances.

Women tend to experience a more severe economic drop after divorce than men, for two main reasons. Men usually contribute the majority to the family finances, so without this input, women hurt more financially. Secondly, women usually end up assuming the lion's share of child-rearing, which means they must bear these costs largely on their own.

We know that one of the key triggers of divorce is financial pressure. It may be the pressure of both parents having to work and not having enough time for each other. It might be the pressure of one person staying at home so there is never enough money to enjoy life or be able to give the opportunities you want to your kids. It could be because you and your partner have different and incompatible money personalities, or a lack of financial direction, so are aimless. There are many drivers of financial frustration. What we do know, though, is that the middle class (of which there are many) are likely to require two earners to sustain the lifestyle they want to live and the opportunities they want to give their children. This could cause fallout, and if there is fallout, it is more likely that the female will be more adversely affected financially.

Most parents, whether they are working or not, recognise the value of investing their time in their kids' lives. I was comforted to find that parents today spend at least as much time with their children as they did in the mid-1960s, when most families followed the stay-at-home-mum model. True, women are spending much less time on housework (thankfully), but their overall time with their children has remained remarkably stable and may actually have risen slightly.

Men, by contrast, are clearly spending more time with their children than they used to—more than a third more (although still substantially less than women). In balancing work and family, parents have largely preserved the precious time with their children that is so crucial. What they have sacrificed, though, is time with each other and their communities, time spent doing housework, time for themselves and time sleeping.

However, in families where both parents have to work, you don't need to despair. Research by the Harvard Business School shows there are significant benefits for children growing up with mothers who work outside the home. The study found daughters of working mothers went to school longer, were more likely to have a job in a supervisory role and earned 23 per cent more than their peers who were raised by stay-at-home mothers. The sons of working mothers also tended to pitch in more on household chores and childcare!

WOMEN AND MONEY

It is a generally accepted belief that nurturing is a basic instinct to women. We are also taught to give of ourselves. We take care of our family, our friends, the wider community. Yet we are slower to take care of our money than most other things in our life that we care about.

A lot of women I coach start to engage with money because they can no longer refuse to—as opposed to doing it by preference. It seems many women prefer to leave money and its role in relationships to the side. We learn this from a young age, usually from a parent who does not deem it necessary to discuss or develop financial skills with their daughters to the same extent they would their sons. Studies have shown that 23 per cent of parents take the time to discuss ways to invest money and grow wealth with their sons, compared to 13 per cent who discuss this with their daughters. An annual 'Parents, Kids & Money' survey in the US by T. Rowe Price showed that girls trail boys in markets of financial fluency. The gender gap starts at home, when it comes to discussing finances and feeling confident about money matters, according to *Baltimore Business Journal*.

As a result of either low financial confidence or ignorance, women often don't want to embrace money until they need to and there is no other option but to confront money matters. Until that point they don't apply to money that same primal, nurturing impulse that they extend to every other aspect of their lives.

Our relationship with money reflects our relationship with ourselves. If you are the kind of woman who puts everyone and everything before yourself, often at your own expense, this attitude can extend to how you handle money (and to a possible lack of career progression). Financial planner and author Suze Orman goes so far as to say that if you don't have a healthy relationship with money then you don't value yourself—which is applicable to both males and females.

On the one hand, women have come so far, so fast in the workplace in the last two generations. But we have failed to make the same evolutionary leap when it comes personal finances. Many women are yet to conclude that looking after themselves means looking after their money, and vice versa.

Women today make up nearly half the total workforce. They contribute to almost half of families' incomes, and female-owned businesses are on the rise, at 44 per cent in New Zealand (and 40 per cent in the US), according to a press release issued by MYOB in October 2016. Over the last 30 years the cultural and social change has been impressive. Ignoring the glass ceilings and old boys' clubs, as a social class we have come so far.

However, what these impressions of progress do not show is that more than 90 per cent of women feel insecure when it comes to their finances. A 2006 survey commissioned by Allianz Insurance in the US found nearly half the respondents (all women) said that the prospects of ending up in poverty had crossed their minds at some point. Further studies suggest that women are nearly twice as likely as men to retire poor.

In a 2009 report on female economic behaviour and spending, researchers found that the most common reason women go on a shopping spree is to cheer themselves up. This is not to say that females are more likely to be 'shoppers' than men, because that is not the case. But alarmingly, when stressed and seeking comfort, eight out of ten women surveyed said this was why they shopped, as spending money made them feel in control. They didn't necessarily spend a lot of money or purchase a lot of things. But little treats are still treats and when stressed many women feel they need them (myself included). Interestingly, one-third of the same group also felt guilt or shame over a shopping trip.

As a parent, I know what makes you feel worse is knowing that your kids are watching you. If you go shopping every time you are stressed, then they are going to think that is what you do. No matter what you say about money, they will get the message loud and clear that the only way to be happy or get over a bad mood is to go out and spend money.

WHAT TO TELL OUR DAUGHTERS

In my day job, I meet many smart women who have accomplished so much. As a social class, we would all agree that women have made huge inroads. But the painful truth is that for all the advancements women have made, too little has changed in the way women deal with money and the share of the load at home. What goes on behind closed doors is still 'old school' and not transferrable to the environment our daughters will need to survive in.

This wouldn't be too much of an issue if women could bank on relationships sticking and their life partner doing what was needed to ensure the family unit ended up where it needed to be. But for our daughters this is more of an issue, because the reliance on security from a partner has eroded further. Being a working mum will be the norm, as most families will not be able to afford to have one parent staying at home (well, not if they want to own the home they live in).

This is not to say that females should expect the worst, but on some level we resign ourselves to accepting average when it comes to our financial wellbeing. Too many women do not take control of their financial status. All too often I see broken relationships where the woman is not in a position to do what is needed because their financial status and position is too weak.

Many women in second marriages, or with significantly more assets than their spouse, are not protecting the wealth they bring to the relationship. Females are more likely than males to intermingle inheritances into the family finances, and lose it to relationship property claims. I can't count the number of times I have seen this, and it breaks my heart. These women feel uncomfortable discussing money issues with their new partners.

Too often I see intelligent women turning a blind eye to the financial inequality of a relationship, in the name of keeping the peace. I understand that it is ultimately their decision, but what message is this showing their children, especially their daughters? It's dysfunctional and damaging. How is this teaching our sons to respect women as equals when this financial disparity exists at home?

With the challenges that our children are likely to face, and the lack of security being offered to females compared to previous generations, the need to teach our daughters and equip them with the tools for success is crucial, to attempt to make the playing field more even. And if they have no point of reference to be financially strong for themselves, where are they supposed to learn this? To protect themselves, they need to learn these skills well before they might need to put them into practice. They need to learn this from their parents, while at home, to avoid developing a dysfunctional relationship with money.

How to be a successful giver

Generosity is a quality that women can tap into easily, possibly too easily. At times we give for the sake of giving, which can be a nice quality, but if you give more than you can afford, consistently—well, that is just stupid.

When I challenge my clients on this, they say one of the

reasons why they give is that they don't know how to give less. They feel guilty if they give less.

Too many girls go through life trying to be pleasers. So much of their life, decisions and security is based around pleasing others, at their own expense. This is unsustainable and not what it means to be a successful giver.

In life, you are either a giver, a taker or a matcher. A giver gives more than they receive, a taker takes more than they give, and a matcher matches what they give with what they take. In his book *Give and Take: Why Helping Others Drives Our Success*, Adam Grant shows that givers sink to the bottom of the success ladder because they make others better off by sacrificing their own success or advancement.

This in itself isn't too surprising. But what is fascinating is that givers also make up the top of the success ladder, with takers and matchers in the middle. Successful givers are willing to ask for help and are every bit as ambitious as non-givers but have a different way of pursuing their goals.

Unsuccessful givers are what author and professor at Oakland University Barbara Oakley describes as being pathologically selfless, when the giving has an unhealthy focus on others, to your own detriment. Giving so much of your money away that you fail to achieve your financial goals is a sign of pathological selflessness. These types can become pushovers and usually end up exhausted. Selfless giving, in the absence of self-preservation, can become overwhelming and unsustainable.

According to Grant, successful givers 'care about benefiting others, but they also have ambitious goals for advancing their own interests . . . [it] means being willing to give more than you receive, but still keeping your own interests in sight, using them as a guide for choosing when, where, how and to whom you give.'

When concern for others is coupled with a good dose of concern for yourself, then you are less prone to getting burnt out or being taken advantage of. You are less likely to avoid the pitfalls of being a failed giver.

We all need to bear this in mind, but especially females, who may struggle to balance the needs of self with the needs of others, especially as it relates to money.

CONCLUSION

To nurture others and to give of ourselves are two wonderful traits that come more naturally to some than to others, and, it seems, comes more naturally to females than to males. If giving is something you wish to encourage in your children, then make sure the lesson is tempered with examples of how to give successfully and not at the expense of your own financial wellbeing. Your daughters will most likely face more financial challenges than your sons will, so prepare them for this. Get them ready through conversation, by sharing the workload at home fairly, by giving equal pay for chores, and equal opportunity to complete different jobs. Take the time to explain and illustrate how financial success can be achieved without a future partner, and how, once it's achieved, it must be protected. Equip your children for success by helping them to identify the challenges they are likely to face and how to push through them, with their health, relationship and finances still intact.

CHAPTER 10
18–22: LEAVING THE NEST

My parents gave me the gift of believing I could do anything I wanted if I set my mind to it and was prepared to work hard enough. My dad used to say, 'Work hard for five years, Hannah, so you can have fifty years of easy.' I have since concluded that five years is probably more like 20. But if you are doing something you enjoy, or know that what you are doing will help you get something you enjoy, you don't begrudge the journey.

Objectives:
- They have a plan to minimise the amount of debt they take on while studying.
- They know where their degree is taking them. Is it going to allow them to live the life they want?
- They understand what employers are looking for and how

they can position themselves in the best light.
- Understands that money underpins everything.
- Understands the traits of successful people.
- Actively saves and invests (if not at university).
- Shows economic self-sufficiency and can live on a budget.
- Understands how the banking system works and what caused the GFC.

Key conversations:
- The world is changing, which means our kids need to be faster, better, smarter. But what does that actually mean?
- Don't get a useless degree.
- Explain the things that you regret you did, or the things you are pleased you have done as a parent.

PAYING FOR YOUR KIDS' EDUCATION—SHOULD YOU DO IT?

A lot of parents ask me if they should pay for their kids' education, or if they should at the very least contribute to their education costs. The answer is yes you should, if you can and it's important to you. If you can't or it's not, then you shouldn't.

How do you know if you can afford it? Firstly, you need to be sure your own retirement is sorted before you get too generous with your kids. Secondly, start saving for their education only when you are financially ready. To be financially ready means that you are out of debt (with the exception of your mortgage), you have a full emergency fund to cover six months of living costs and you are contributing a minimum of 10 per cent towards saving for your retirement (although some financial advisors may suggest 15 per cent—the exact amount differs depending on how much you need and how long you have to save it). It is only at that point that you should entertain the notion of saving for your kids' education.

This can be an uncomfortable pill to swallow, especially for parents who feel that without saving for their kids' education they are a 'bad' parent. If you can help your kids and save for retirement then that is great, but you will retire and there is only one way to sort your retirement, and that is by starting a growth strategy today.

Paying for your kids' education is only one way to help your kids. You could give them free board while they are studying, help them into their first home or send them 'Red Cross' packages while they are away. You could invest in a financial coach to help them develop a strategy and support to get them to where they need to be. Or you help them by being honest about your financial failings and lessons. Non-monetary assistance can be just as powerful as a handout.

In reality it will always come down to what is the most important thing to you at the time. You can often manipulate your budget to accommodate the things you want to do or have. I have worked with some parents who are spending a lot of money on their lifestyle, because they haven't previously had a reason not to. But then something happens, either a curve ball or the realisation that their kids are going to be doing it harder than they did and they have not imparted to them the financial wisdom they had hoped. Suddenly 'helping them through university' becomes the most important thing to them.

I work with these parents to redevelop their spending plan to accommodate this desire—and their retirement. The thing that is ultimately cut back is the lifestyle the parents are prepared to live. The willingness to make these concessions stems from a strong desire to aid their children.

I personally don't think that parents incurring debt to save their kids from incurring debt is the way to go—although for some of my clients that is what they choose. We have to work pretty hard to neutralise this decision, so it doesn't have a disastrous effect on the parents' finances. The detrimental effect of bailing your kid out can be felt for some time—as evidenced by this generation of millennials.

One study that did surprise me showed that paying for your kids' college education doesn't always translate to giving them a leg up. The study by Laura Hamilton of the University of California, Merced found that parents who fund their child's education do increase that child's chances of attending college, as well as their odds of graduating, but parents' financial support actually decreases a student's grades. Paying for your kids' education usually means they show up to class, but not perform as well as they would if they paid for the classes themselves. The study found that as parental aid increased, every income group saw a reduction in GPA (grade point average)—with the curve steepest among the most privileged students. The chart on the next page shows the striking results.

Hamilton concluded that the effects of parental financial support on grades was modest overall and not enough to decrease a student's odds of graduating, but 'any reduction in student GPA due to parental aid—which is typically offered with the best of intentions—is both surprising and important'.

Hamilton suspects the reason behind the drop is that students who receive endless financial support from Mum and Dad may not take their education as seriously as those students who have to weigh up the financial investment and return of university. She also found after interviewing parents that students also had

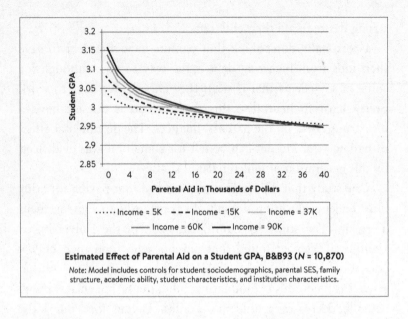

Estimated Effect of Parental Aid on a Student GPA, B&B93 (N = 10,870)

Note: Model includes controls for student sociodemographics, parental SES, family structure, academic ability, student characteristics, and institution characteristics.

lower grades if their parents not only paid for their schooling but also did not discuss the students' own responsibility for their education.

CHOOSING A MAJOR—DON'T LET YOUR KIDS DO A USELESS DEGREE

Take a common-sense approach to picking a major. Your child should study something that interests them, in a field that offers jobs at the end, at an income level and with job progression that will help them transition to financial independence as quickly as possible. Please do not abandon your child to choose a degree without your input, and without you connecting them with people who work in the field so they can get a better sense of what is involved. I have seen too many parents and kids endorse or complete a useless degree. Parents want to support their kids, because the idea of contradicting their child's passion would be frowned upon, and kids justify this course because they are passionate about it.

Among the hundreds of kids I interviewed while researching this book, the main reason for choosing a course was that they were passionate about the subject. I asked all of the kids if they knew what the job was that they were likely to do when they graduated and how much it would pay. I asked if they knew how much they needed to earn to live the lifestyle they think they want to live—which, let's assume, was on par with their parents. Less than 15 per cent had any true idea.

GIVING YOUR KIDS PURPOSE

All kids need a part-time job and should be encouraged to work through university. Most of the parents I work with freak out at this point—at which point I ask them to bring their teenager to our next meeting. The most common objections are:

- My child's grades will suffer if they work.
- I want my kid to enjoy university.

I hear this rhetoric from teenagers and tertiary students as well. When I interviewed one group of Year 12 students, one of them told me that he wanted to focus on his schoolwork and working part time would be a distraction from that. I asked if he was serious. He said yes. I burst out laughing. I mean, come on. A part-time job will not hurt your child's grades. Studies show that it actually improves them for students who work between 10 and 15 hours per week, compared to those students who don't hold a job.

What we know is that 'There is not enough time to do all the nothing we want to do' (a quote by cartoonist Bill Watterson, creator of *Calvin and Hobbes*). According to one *New York Times* article, American university students watch on average 24 hours of internet or TV a week, more than the average person. You could tell your kid that you are prepared to help them at university but they need to compromise some of their TV-watching time to help pay the bills. According to the American Psychiatry Association, 40 per cent of college students also 'drink heavily'. The need and opportunity to hold down a part-time job to help pay for tertiary education can cut down the amount of time wasted and help them develop strong time-management skills.

If you are rocking up to your future employer and you say that you worked two jobs during university and graduated without a student loan, versus another student who didn't work and has a student loan, which student do you think the future employer is going to be more impressed with? Many employers claim that students who have worked part time during school and university exhibit more sophisticated life skills and better judgement.

One study commissioned by UPromise, an American organisation which helps people accrue savings to pay for education through loyalty programmes, found that working a limited number of hours (e.g. 10–15) appears to have a positive impact on student performance. A 1993 report published in the *Journal of Student Financial Aid* studied college-student employment and its effect on the GPA scores of participants. And here is the crazy thing. Students who worked 11–20 hours per week reported a higher average GPA than students who didn't work at all. Weirder still, students who worked full time while studying full time reported the same average grades as students who didn't work at all. Those who worked part time (up to 20 hours per week) showed a higher average mark than those who didn't work at all.

The tipping point for what constitutes too much work is anything above 35 hours, but this is where it gets interesting (or disturbing). Another study surveyed 30,000 college freshmen from 76 colleges and universities in the US. Students were asked to report on how much time they spent drinking, and how often. And how much time did the average student spend drinking and socialising each week?

10.2 hours.

The researchers then asked students to estimate how much time was spent each week on a handful of other activities. Here are the results:

Studying: 8.4 hours

Exercising: 5 hours

Online social-networking and video games: 4 hours

Working for pay: 2.5 hours

By eliminating online socialisation and cutting their drinking time in half, there is at least nine hours of newly available time that can be used for working for pay. Cut the TV-watching in half, and you have another 12 hours. You can easily find 10 to 15 hours of time for work. This still allows time for a full-time university workload, exercise, a generous amount of TV-watching and surfing the net, and a chunk of drinking time.

FIGHT TO MINIMISE THE STUDENT LOAN

For whatever reason, you may prefer your child did not work while at university. But if your child is going to be taking out a student loan, they must be encouraged to work before taking out a loan for their living costs.

If your kids are living at home and you are not charging board, they do not need a living allowance from a student loan. They should be strongly encouraged to work part time to cover their basic living costs. They should be encouraged to work during the holidays to save to cover their course fees.

University is not a free ride. It is an expensive route that should be treated like most other debts. If you don't feel the pain upfront, it almost doesn't register that a cost has been chalked up. But it does add up and it adds up fast. Your job is to teach your child to minimise the cost and work hard to get rid of it as soon as possible.

CONCLUSION

Leaving the nest is such an exciting time for teenagers, yet for their parents it can be heart-rending. My mum once said that when I left home it felt like a death to her, and I certainly felt like the prodigal child when I returned at the end of every semester. Our babies will always be our babies, but at eighteen they have grown up. Among other things, they have the option of choosing a course of study that they hope will eventually provide them with a job in a field they will enjoy. This opportunity to learn about and to tailor a career path through study is just one of the wonders of university—many students will find themselves exposed to things they might never have known before. Their eyes will be opened and, if they are lucky, they'll discover a career that they want to move towards.

However, many students go to university with no clear idea of what they will come out with or the trade it will allow. This is not new, but what *is* new is the level of debt that now accompanies tertiary study. There is too little attention paid to the career options a degree offers, and even less attention is given to the student loans that are often required to study. Your job as a parent is to guide your child to understand that university study includes part-time work, and that a student loan is the last option *not* the first when it comes to supplementing income. The extent to which your child incurs student-loan debt is largely in their hands, but it's important to instil in them well before they embark on tertiary study the idea that student-loan debt should be minimised, no matter what.

CHAPTER 11
23–30: TAKING FLIGHT

If your kids attend university straight out of high school, they will graduate in their early twenties. Graduation is where the rubber hits the road and real life kicks in. If your child has incurred a student loan to study something they no longer like or in an industry lacking jobs, then they need to change tack and identify another profession as quickly as possible. This might be challenging, but it is not impossible. What happens between the ages of 23 and 30 will set your child's financial course for the next 20 years of their life.

Objectives:
- They have a plan to be able to pay off their student loan within four years of graduation, or in the same amount of time they accrued it. (This is not to say they will actually

pay it off, but they should at least be in a position to do so.)

- They are in a position to buy a house by no later than the age of 30 (26 if you rattle your dags and prove yourself a 'good bet').
- They have a financial strategy in place.
- They understand the things that make them happy and make sure they have enough time and money to do these, while ensuring points one and two can be achieved.
- They know who is going to be in their 'team' to help them get ahead faster.
- They are able to move on after financial mistakes.

Key conversations:
- When they find their life partner, make sure they share the same financial goals.
- Understanding the money personality of your spouse.
- Understanding how to get paid what you are worth.

HOW TO GET RID OF A STUDENT LOAN

The best way to pay off a student loan is not to get one, or at the very least to minimise the size of the loan.

This can be more challenging if your kid has to move away from home to study. But if they were to work every holiday and 10 hours a week during term time, earning $18 per hour, it is possible for them to fund their university education without a student loan. Certainly, they will not be buying new clothes and their budget for beer will be lower than most—but can it be done? Yes. If you are not in a position to help your kids go to university, then it's not a case of should they try to self-fund their education, but more a case of 'they need to'.

The average annual cost of attending a university where you must pay accommodation and board is $20,000 (including tuition). University runs for 32 weeks of the year. During this time, your kid works 15 hours per week. They want (and probably need) at least four weeks of holiday each year, so of the 20 free weeks, they can work full time for 16 of them. Basic arithmetic suggests that they could earn approximately $8000 gross during term time and $11,500 during the holidays. Of course, tax needs to be deducted from these numbers, but you can see that a student loan does not need to be a certainty and shouldn't be encouraged as the first obvious choice for kids. Your kids will need to be used to working before university for this to be a viable option, however.

Too many students who might have their hostel fees covered or live at home opt to receive the student loan to cover their living costs. One might ask what that would be for, if their accommodation and board is covered? It's basically free money to spend how they want—up to $176 per week. Kids love it, their friends are getting it, and they can get it as well. One small catch—you have to pay it back.

If all your basic living costs are covered, having $176 per week to spend as you see fit (on entertainment, drinking, etc.) is a lot of money. It's more than what some of my adult clients have to spend at their leisure each week! Do I think the government should pay it out as freely as they do? No. Although there will be some genuine instances where that money is used for true living costs—but too many kids get the money and spend it like it is their own and it doesn't have to be repaid. Educate your kids on this before they have a line of credit of $176 per week.

For those who end up with a student loan, whether it was

avoidable or unavoidable, you now need to work out how to get rid of it. The goal is to set aside enough money each year so that you can repay it within three to four years of graduating.

Student-loan repayments are not deducted from the first $19,084 of income earned, but every dollar earned after that has 12 cents put towards repayment. If the average graduate salary is $35,000, then $1900 of the money earned each year will go towards repaying your loan. This makes the loan repayment long and arduous. If your student loan was $40,000 and you are repaying just under $2000 per year, it is going to take you 10–15 years to repay the loan (this assumes your income increases over time so your repayments increase to repay the loan sooner).

To repay the loan in four years, if $2000 a year is being directly deducted, you need to save a further $8000 each year to be on track. If this feels too hard, or the income earned is too low to cover living costs and debt repayment, then learn this fact before you do the degree. Delay university by a year or two and save for it. Teach your kids to respect the severity of the student loan before it overshadows them.

MOVING HOME AFTER UNIVERSITY

To help your kids get rid of their loan sooner, consider letting them move back home to allow them to save faster—but make sure they do, otherwise you need to kick them out. Too often I see adult children living at home and not contributing to living costs. It is frustrating and a disservice to your kids. Respect them enough to charge them for their living costs. I encourage all the parents I work with to charge board as soon as their child graduates (which is at least three months after finishing university).

The only exception to living at home after university for free is if your kid doesn't have a job (but is actively looking for one), or if they are saving for something and can verify or prove their savings plan. If they are working, they must pay board.

Parents, $50 per week is not board. It is an insult. It should be a minimum of $150–$200 per week. They would have to spend at least twice that if they moved out and flatted with friends.

A lot of parents struggle with the idea of taking money from their children to live at home. Take it. You are doing them a favour and teaching them about the big bad world they should have transitioned to.

I would prefer the money you receive is used to cover the costs of keeping your adult child at home. But I couldn't care less if you deposit it in a separate (and secret) account that you intend to give back to your kids in the future. What you use the money for is not the issue here; the point is that if you overly minimise your kids' obligations, it usually just means they spend more on themselves, instead of getting ahead faster.

LIVING AT HOME—HOW TO STOP IT

As a parent, having your child not live with you for the rest of your life should be the most basic of goals. Your job is to raise an arrow, not a boomerang.

While it can make sound financial sense for your child to live at home, especially if it is going to allow them to repay their student loan faster or save for a house sooner, these examples tend to be the minority. Most of the adult children still living at home do so because it is easier and means they have more money to spend on themselves, so why wouldn't they? It is not a wealth strategy; it is a spending strategy that should be seen for what it really is—'failure to launch'. These kids are allowed to confuse a safety net for a hammock.

Of course, certain conditions require you to offer a place of refuge for your kid. But if it is translating to them refusing to look for a job, staying out late, sleeping later, not doing their own laundry or making their own food—then you have spoiled your child.

If you agree that your child can move home because of financial setbacks (loss of job, etc.), you set the conditions. Firstly, it is for an agreed period, and not in perpetuity. I don't think that they need to pay board if there is a crisis, but they need to be modelling behaviour to change their situation.

One suggestion by American author Dave Ramsey is instead of paying rent, you might require them to be job hunting for three hours per day, or to complete a budget and show you.

Safety nets do save you, but they are not meant to be comfortable. If your child is receiving an unemployment benefit, at least half of this should be paid to you as board.

Buying your property—how to do it

Many millennials I spoke to didn't see the point in owning their own home. It seemed unattainable and provided little value to them. (This was true for millennials from across the country, but was more strongly felt in the major centres of Auckland, Wellington and Christchurch.) I would hope by the time you have worked with your child through the key objectives of each chapter in this book that it will be clear that getting on the property ladder is the single most important step for your child if they want to fast-track wealth creation (on the assumption that they buy the right property in the right area). To recap its importance:

- You only need to come up with 20 per cent of the property's value.
- You can leverage from the bank.
- You can use your KiwiSaver to contribute to the deposit and may qualify for other grants.
- If you have a shortfall you may be able to access the equity in your parents' home to assist you.
- You can go in with a partner (parents or friend), or form a syndicate of people (the fewer the better), owning the property jointly.
- You can improve the property's value with your own efforts.
- You can have flatmates who will pay your mortgage for you.

It is likely the first home you buy will be at the lower end of the purchase-price spectrum, which means that any corrections in the property market are unlikely to affect that property since it will be purchased for its replacement value (i.e. you won't be able to build it any cheaper).

The residential property market tends to increase in value over a property cycle, which ranges from every eight to 14 years, depending on the location and the type of the property. For example, properties in Auckland tend to increase in value faster than properties in Invercargill. Over a property cycle, properties fluctuate in value, although on average they often double in value over a set period. But the property market does not consistently increase in value. It goes up, and then it comes down. There are times when there is unprecedented growth, shortly followed by 'the bottom falling out of the market', which basically means that, if you had to sell a property at that point, you might be forced to sell it for less than you purchased it for. (The idea, of course, is to position yourself so that you do not need to do this.)

While a property can drop in value, this exposure is usually capped at what it would cost to replace a basic dwelling on the same property. Properties where the land value is high have the most potential to fall when a property market corrects; by comparison, cheaper properties have a smaller risk of reductions because they are buffered by the fact there are no cheaper substitutes. In other words, you couldn't build the property any cheaper, so the property value is linked to actual costs as opposed to market or perceived value.

One of the benefits of buying your first home as young as possible is that your tastes are more in keeping with what a first home needs to be. Your first home isn't supposed to be brand new, have all the modern conveniences or be in a great location. It's supposed to be a bit of a dive and need some work. It doesn't need to be in the best neighbourhood, but you don't want to buy in the Bronx if you can help it, as the capital gain is likely to take longer.

You need to look at the historical capital gain in the area where you are purchasing. Research the rate of growth and how long it takes for gains to be made. Understand what the council are doing and whether people are likely to be moving to the area in the future, as that will help push up its value.

Give yourself a budget and a year to do it up. Work on the property in the weekends, and at night. Put every cent you earn towards reducing the mortgage or funding the cost of renovation. Go hard for 12 months.

Once it is finished, speak to the local real estate agent to see what the property is worth. If they think it is worth more than $50,000 more than when you first purchased it, get a registered valuation to verify this. Go back to the bank and tell them the property has gone up in value (showing them the registered valuation), and ask to increase your mortgage to 80 per cent of the new property value. This will be higher than what you initially borrowed. The difference can then be used as a deposit for your next property. If the extra amount you can access is insufficient for you to buy a property (because it doesn't amount to 20 per cent of the new property's purchase price), then you have the options of:

- waiting for your property to increase in value further
- buying the second property with someone else
- getting a second mortgage to cover the deposit shortfall, or
- buying a property off the plans with a long settlement, backing yourself to come up with (either through saving or future capital gains) the difference needed to purchase the second property.

It is best that you work with a financial advisor to make sure you adopt the right strategy, recognising that not all properties are good investment properties. You need to get advice on the right property for you, but the conceptual process can be understood without detailing the exact characteristics of the preferred property, which will differ for each person involved.

When I work with parents and their kids on this strategy they feel equal parts excitement and nervousness. In my experience, you feel more comfortable when you have access to all the information you need to make an informed decision, and an independent sounding board to bounce ideas, strategies and concerns off. For a lot of the people I work with, we have one shot to get it right, as there is no financial leeway if we get it wrong.

GETTING ON THE PROPERTY LADDER TOGETHER— COMBINING FINANCIAL INTERESTS

When it comes to owning property, unless there is a good reason not to, you should always try to 'own it yourself', so that you are the sole owner of the asset. This is cleaner and usually the preferred option. It comes with risks—namely, the buck stops with you for everything—but the capital gain is all yours.

But sometimes you can't afford the property by yourself and sometimes pulling together with a partner can give you access to more, sooner. In addition to this, joining forces with someone can be a good solution to overcome financial setbacks, allowing you to share the deposit requirements, servicing obligations, property improvement workload as well as general support. The cost of having a partner is the sharing of the gain, but if having a partner or not is the difference between owning the property or not, then it makes sense to have one.

The question, though, is who should that partner be? In my view, usually the best partner for your child will be you, their parent—because usually your goals are more aligned and you are not going to rip your child off (I would hope). My preference for a parent assisting their child with property ownership is for them to also have a stake in the property, so the hoped-for capital gain will benefit the child and the parent. This could be of significant value to a parent who owns their home, but has insufficient funds for retirement. The capital gain on an investment property, over a 10- to 15-year period, may be all they need to fill their retirement gap. If it also helps their child get on to the property ladder, then it can kill two birds.

As a parent, you need to first understand what your retirement gap is, and what other investment options are available to you, so you know the decision to buy a property is the right one for you. Because of the smaller deposit requirements and the ability to leverage using the bank's money, it can work well, however.

Another option for a parent wanting to position themselves to be able to assist their kids in the future at a low entry-cost is to buy an investment property earmarked for your kids' future, separate to your own retirement assets. Using the equity in your home as the deposit, you buy the investment, likely topping it up each week to cover the shortfall in rent and property costs. Ideally you would buy this property before your children are 15. This gives the property 10 years to increase in value (hopefully) before you might need to access the capital gain for student-loan repayments or to help your children leverage to buy a property for themselves.

Not all properties are good properties, however, and from my study of the market, normally 10 per cent or less of the properties advertised are going to be a good investment property. But assuming you work to strict criteria (that you can find on my website, www.enableme.co.nz), this can be an effective way of creating wealth for the direct benefit of your kids.

Let's say you purchased a $350,000 property. It costs you $100 per week in top-ups. You have to own the property for 15 years before you get a capital gain. Let's say it increases in value to $650,000 in this time. You have had to pay $78,000 in top-ups (which you need to view as a form of compulsory savings), but you have made a gain of $300,000. Less the $78,000 you have topped it up by, this means that you have made $222,000 from holding the property. You might then choose to sell the property to pay for your kids' education or as a deposit for their first home.

I have oversimplified this process, but you get the gist of what you are trying to do and how. When assisting my clients with this, we go through all the implications (pros and cons) and the property criteria they need to look for, so that they are comfortable that the investment selected is right for their situation. Too many people get burnt with property because they think that any old property will do. In the good times this is true, but in the bad times (and you get them every property cycle), it's a killer.

First: is your retirement sorted?

Before you can assist your kids with tertiary studies, you need to know your own retirement is sorted. Take the time to work through this. If you are unsure if your retirement is on track, there are some quick questions you can answer to get an idea if there is going to be a shortfall.

What is the term of your mortgage, or how long before your mortgage is repaid in full? (This will show on your loan statements.) How old will you be when your mortgage is repaid? If you will be older than 65, you cannot afford to help your kids and you really need to help yourself—quickly! If you are on track to be mortgage-free before retirement, you need to be able to answer the following three questions.

1. How many years do you have between being mortgage-free and retiring?
2. What do you currently save each year?
3. What are your annual mortgage repayments?

Multiply the amount you save each year (2) by the number of years between now and when you retire (1). Then add to this amount your annualised mortgage payments (3) multiplied by the number of years you are mortgage-free before retirement. This will give you the total approximate savings you will accumulate before you retire (a), without factoring in KiwiSaver.

Next, you need to account for any less regular income or expenses events, and you also need to factor in KiwiSaver. First off, what big costs are you facing between now and retirement? For example, do you intend to complete house renovations, car replacements, big holidays, dental work, or give 'gifts' to the kids. Add all of these things together, then deduct the total from the approximate savings you worked out earlier (a).

Next, add any one-off instances of income you might receive, for example, downsizing the house or selling investments. Some people might also include likely inheritances; others might prefer not to.

Finally, add your KiwiSaver to the running total.

This final amount is what you are likely to have saved by retirement at the rate you are currently chugging along at. We will call this your 'total savings'.

Now we need to ascertain how long that amount will last. This is where things can get a little complicated, as you need to know what your living costs are each year, excluding mortgage payments. Multiply your current living costs by 80 per cent, as we work to a rule of thumb that you will spend 20 per cent less in retirement than you currently do. The answer to this equation is what we will call your 'retirement lifestyle'.

Divide your 'total savings' by your 'retirement lifestyle' to find out how many years your savings will last into retirement. The goal is to have amassed total savings to fund 25 years of retirement.

If your total savings will last for less than 25 years, then you will likely face a problem that will require a strategy to fix. If you are not going to be mortgage-free by retirement, then you need a more aggressive strategy to fix things. So get to it.

A lot of parents reading this book will need a retirement strategy because they are not going to have saved enough to live on once retired. Most of these people will know this intuitively without having to go through the calculations above. The great thing about recognising this is that you can collaborate with your child to help them to help you. It's a circular win for all, if done right.

As a side note, when investing together, it usually pays to have a third party facilitate the agreement to the terms of the contract. The failing of families working together is often that the arrangement is treated too casually. If you are entering into a business relationship with anyone, it needs to be run like a non-familial transaction, so that all parties are aware of what is required and how the agreement might fail.

My team and I run workshops with parents and their adult children around how to master this process and navigate around the common pitfalls of working with your family. When someone independent and qualified comments, you get away with saying things that might not have been so readily accepted if said between related parties.

FINDING A PARTNER—A FATAL ATTRACTION?

As noted in earlier chapters, financial stress is the leading cause of relationship breakdowns. One of the more obvious areas of pressure comes from financial incompatibility.

Studies show that we have certain tendencies when it comes to finding a mate that extend to money personalities. If you are more middle of the road in your money personality (more of a plodder than an extreme shopper or a saver), much research suggests that 'birds of a feather flock together', meaning you will feel attracted to people who do have a similar personality to you. If you have an extreme personality, you will most likely be more attracted to those who don't possess similar characteristics to yours in a bid to offset a perceived shortcoming in yourself.

Deborah Small of the University of Michigan and her co-authors found that tightwads, who generally spend less than they would like to spend, and spendthrifts, who generally spend more than they would like to spend, tend to marry each other. Despite the shared and complementary attraction, these differences in tendencies (tightwad versus spendthrift) predict conflict over finances. As we know, conflict over finances within any relationship predicts diminished marital wellbeing. No great surprises there!

When your kid is young and in love they might not pick up on the financial differences between them and their potential life partner—but you as parents will. It might please you or make you nervous. You might choose to voice your opinion or keep it to yourself. But where your views will be really tested is if your kid then wants you to lend them money.

Lending money to your kids when you don't like their partner

Irrespective of whether or not you like your kid's life partner, if you are in position to be generous with your kids, perhaps with helping them with a deposit for their first home, be sure to protect your child's interests first. Relationship property law suggests that once you live in a de facto relationship for three years, all property can become joint in the event you later separate. This makes sense, but is seldom equitable if only one side of the relationship has given money to the partnership.

As a parent, I feel that I would probably have a bit to say if I thought my child's partner was bad news. I would still want my child to do well and if I was able, I would still give what I have to give them a head-start. But I wouldn't just 'give' anything. I would document the money advanced as a loan, in a deed (of acknowledgement of debt) that I would have both spouses sign. I might not require the money back, but the deed would say that in the event of the relationship ending, death or the property being sold, the money lent needs to be repaid.

Alternatively, you could take an interest in the property for the amount of the money lent. For example, if your child and their partner were going to purchase a property for $300,000, and you could lend $60,000, this would give you a 20 per cent interest in the property and you could reflect your name on the title of the property. This way, should they sell the property or later split, you still get your money back, which you would then likely lend back to your child after the separation is finalised.

If you opted for a share of the property, you would also be entitled to the capital gain on that share in the event of a property sale. Again, it is simply an amount ring-fenced from the relationship that is repaid to you, to on-lend back to your child post-separation.

It is best that you assume that any relationship your kids are in might end, and that the money you 'gave' needs to be repaid. The only way to do this is if it is documented as a loan. This could prove challenging in some instances with the bank, where they want any money given by parents to be 'gifted'. If this is the case, I strongly recommend you have your child complete a contracting-out agreement (a 'pre-nup'), specifying the money lent by you will remain separate property in the event of a relationship breakdown. Both your child and their partner will need to sign this, as well as get an independent legal opinion.

In my view, to justify this expense and effort, the amount lent would need to be more than $20,000.

CONCLUSION

Giving your kids a leg up on to the property ladder is a great boost for their financial journey, but make sure you document any advance as a loan or take an interest in the property for the amount lent. Remember that anything you give to your child might inadvertently become relationship property. This means that, if they later separate from a future spouse, your generosity or your child's early inheritance gets halved. It's not particularly romantic, but when it comes to money and family it's prudent to assume the worst and protect yourself and your child's wealth.

If your retirement plan needs a boost, then joining forces with your child to purchase a property might be a way of scratching one another's backs to the financial benefit of all. It comes with challenges and opportunity, and be sure to seek advice when discussing and documenting the arrangement. If you are not in a position to help your child with a deposit or equity, help them in other ways, by facilitating financial advice or introducing them to a team of people who can support them to design a financial strategy that will best suit them.

CONCLUSION

FINANCIAL MILESTONES—FOR PARENTS

As parents, the financial milestones we need to reach are going to be easier than those our kids need to achieve. Currently you can set off on the following path, and you should be OK.

By the age of 30 you should aim to be:
- free of credit-card debt
- making a start on saving for retirement or a house deposit
- have a good credit history
- have repaid your student loan.

By the age of 30–35 you should aim to have:
- purchased a property (doesn't need to be your own home)
- sorted out your financial situation, with a clear understanding of where you are at, what you are up against and the options available to you

- had kids
- survived having kids!

In your forties you should aim to:
- ramp up your retirement savings and develop a retirement strategy
- review your overall financial plan
- if you are going to upgrade your home, do it no later than 50.

In your fifties you should aim to:
- be close to paying off your mortgage
- be completely free of bad debt, e.g. car loans, credit-card debt
- make sure any investments you have are working for you
- understand what your retirement is likely to cost
- understand how much you are likely to have, and what shortfall might exist
- educate yourself around your options to bridge the gap and select a path that will work for you.

In your sixties you should aim to:
- know you are on track to hit your retirement goals
- be able to reduce work hours (after 65) without anxiety.

FINANCIAL MILESTONES FOR OUR KIDS

Our kids need to be starting 10–15 years earlier if they are going to have a shot at a comfortable and enjoyable financial existence.

By the age of 18 you should aim to:
- know what the lifestyle you want to live is likely to cost
- study, take a gap year or enter the workforce

- if you study, know what your student loan is likely to be and what the careers at the other end are likely to pay
- assess whether the investment in a questionable education makes sense
- work to reduce your student-loan size
- not incur other short-term debt, ever.

By the age of 22 you should aim to:
- be graduating and entering the workforce
- determine what level of savings is needed to repay your student loan within four years
- set up a savings account, probably in your parents' name (so that you don't touch it) to build up the funds to repay the student-loan balance (don't pay the loan off unless this is the only wealth-creation option available)
- save 30 per cent of every pay cheque, or more if you are able to live at home
- share your financial plan with your parents—as you are going to need their support for the next few years
- look to work with a financial advisor who is going to help you develop the right strategy for your situation, assisting you to get to where you want to be faster.

By the age of 26 you should aim to:
- be looking to purchase your first property or invest in a business. These are the wealth-creation options that allow you to leverage (grow your base faster than your own efforts alone)
- determine if you will buy the asset with someone else (parents, friends), or on your own. You will probably need assistance of some kind

- get flatmates in and kill the mortgage
- improve the home's value
- revalue 12 months later
- if there is an increase in value, borrow against this to buy your next property. If you can, avoid selling the first property. Hold it and leverage some more.

By the age of 30 you should aim to:
- own two properties or have a thriving business with growth opportunity
- repay your student loan through either saving or the equity in your property that you can borrow against to pay off the cash
- realise that all properties you own prior to 40 are not your dream home; they are stepping stones to get you to your dream home.

By the age of 40 you should aim to:
- have owned and lived in at least three properties
- be settling into a home you can see yourself enjoying.

WHAT DOES THE FUTURE PROMISE?

We can expect higher unemployment—not necessarily a sign that business is down as much as it is a sign that business is transforming. We can expect higher mal-employment, where you are working in a job beneath your skill set. Studies show us that you will earn more if you go to university, but they fail to point out that half the graduates will work in a job beneath their skill set or not related to the field in which they studied. In spite of this they are likely to have a student loan of around $50,000 that they will still be paying off 10 years after graduating.

In 2009, only 31 per cent of adults surveyed in the US between the ages of 20–25 claimed to be earning enough to fund the lifestyle they wanted to live. This is the result of a lack of preparedness that results in young adults incurring debt to fund a lifestyle they can't afford, and parents continuing to foot the bill, usually in the form of free board, at their own expense. This means that our kids take longer to transition to independence— which if time wasn't a commodity wouldn't be an issue, but it is. Parents are trying to buffer kids from their own financial reality, jeopardising their own retirement to continue to support kids who have failed to launch.

This is what we know.

There are fewer children being born each year. Each young worker will support more and more old people who are living for longer. The pension will reduce or possibly not exist, the cost of housing will continue to rise. The gap between rich and poor will grow and smart people will not necessarily get ahead. Income in isolation, without a wealth-creation strategy, will mean that high earners are less likely to 'land on their feet', as was the case in our grandparents' day.

Parents will not be able to fund their own retirement without selling up and moving to a cheaper part of the country, usually away from their kids and grandkids, which tends to be their reason for living in the first place. The rules of wealth that worked for our grandparents are outdated.

In the last 30 years we have experienced an incoming tide. Now the tide is retreating. US super-investor Warren Buffett said that you don't know who is swimming naked until the tide goes out. There are a lot of parents out there who are skinny-dipping! Our kids need to be able to develop a different set of skills to navigate through the financial rips and still catch the wave.

To help our kids we need them to be prepared for what they will face. We need to deliberately practise with them the skills needed to navigate and think strategically about how we can position them for a greater chance of financial success and life success. And how do you acclimatise to a different environment? You get exposed to it. The earlier the better, with each developmental stage having an accompanying financial objective or task to be mastered.

The message that school, media (and Facebook) tell our kids is that heavy lifting is not for people with talent. They say that to get ahead today you simply need to work smarter. Which is kind of true. But what they fail to explain clearly is that when you work smarter, you still work as hard as you have ever worked before, it is just that every morsel of input needs to create a larger amount of output—that is what smarter means.

Our kids cannot afford to be lazy. They must do chores from an early age. They must, as Julie Lythcott-Haims says in her TED Talk 'How to Raise an Adult', comprehend that 'they need to do the work of life in order to be part of life'. Our kids need to be antifragile and possess more grit. They need to be more resilient than us, able to fail and still press on. Our parenting style needs to allow for our kids to become antifragile, to be smart, generous individuals who are able to live the life they want whether they go to university or not.

If your kids go to university, make them work. Please! Help them develop emotional and fluid intelligence to set themselves apart from their peers when looking for a job. Remind yourself that adversity breeds resourcefulness and innovation. Provide financial role models and honesty around your own finances and financial progress. Make sure you have a retirement plan before you start preaching to your child around the importance of money, otherwise the lesson will be lost in the hypocrisy.

A lot of our kids will go to university. University shows them how to learn and is supposed to introduce them to the wider world of career choice. But there is a marketing spin behind the university business model. Each child will need to develop and understand their strategy of where they want to go and have someone supporting them along this path. If their career choice means they will have limited income, then their need to implement wealth-creation strategies faster to offset their low income will become their reality. This in itself is not a bad thing, but discuss the choice, consequence and options with your child—or have someone else do so. Our kids need a real-life wake-up call before they incur $50,000–$80,000 of debt. It is absurd to let a 17-year-old incur this level of debt without understanding the real ramifications of this.

The student loan is the game-changer for the next generation. It is irresponsible of a parent not to explain that this debt may disadvantage their child for the following 10 years of their post-university life. They need to work during the holidays and get connected to the industry they want to work in.

Support your child to get on to the property ladder as quickly as possible. Support comes in the form of a deposit, guaranteeing, buying a property jointly (for mutual gain), allowing your child to live at home (paying board), or paying for their financial coach. Teach them the principles of leverage and how to take advantage of it. If they have a good business idea, surround them with the right people to help take the idea forward faster. Encourage them to be brilliant but tell them that the world does not owe them a favour.

For the thousands of adult clients my team and I have assisted to get in control of their money, kill their mortgage and sort their retirement, the number-one drain or distraction for future planning is the adult child who should be independent, but is not. As a parent, the accepted non-negotiable cost that overrides any retirement goals is to help your kids. The times we live in will see more and more kids struggle to transition into adulthood with financial success.

As we know, there are limited funds available for pensions. Over the next generation, our parents will be forced to use all their equity to fund their own retirement. The government will run out of money, or significantly drop or delay the already meagre state pensions. There will be no inheritance, no head-start or hand up. Our kids will be on their own.

There is a quagmire of obstacles that will need to be navigated through, but we can help them. We need to help them. We need to teach them because no one else will, and as we teach them we will probably learn a few things ourselves. To end up in the same place as their parents, they will need to work twice as hard. The outgoing tide means that financial success is no longer a rite of passage for those who work hard. You have to work smarter, harder, better, and faster than the generations prior.

One of the lessons we learn is that before you know what you can be, sometimes you need to realise what you are not and should not be. Sometimes you must fail. Failure leads to innovation, growth and becoming more agile. (Well, it's supposed to.) It creates necessity, and necessity creates invention.

Agility and adaptability are the most important concepts in the current landscape. They underpin successful entrepreneurship and radicalise the speed of change. Albert Einstein is quoted as saying 'a person who never made a mistake never tried anything new'. The problem, though, is our school system that has housed our little darlings for the last 10–13 years tells our kids how to succeed, and they measure success by passing exams. This does not translate to the real world on any meaningful level. The system is not designed to help our kids flourish after school ends.

Certainly, teenagers can be selfish, that's part of growing up. But there is a group who want to do well. They are just not sure how to do it. Like their peers, they have been taught to think critically, which means if you are going to teach them they want you want to be sure that you can back up your claims with fact, research or proven examples, otherwise they are not buying into it. This is possibly where most parents tap out because it feels hard, and it is hard. Your children need role models, both in life and in their chosen fields.

Genetics, biases and family environments influence our financial behaviour. Tendencies need to be identified early so that they can be cultivated or further skills developed to offset against weaknesses or taking advantage of opportunities. Each development stage has skills that must be learned to ensure your child is prepared for life after school.

Our girls need to be taught about money differently, as they will usually start disadvantaged. Giving is good, unless it is bad. Be a successful giver, so you can teach your children (and especially daughters) to avoid the pitfalls of trying to please others, all the time. To give successfully is to be generous but not at your own expense or advancement.

Our financial landscape is moving fast and our kids are getting left behind. There is no longer a 'call to arms': instead, we are left to find our way at the rate we want.

This book will help you equip your child for the real world, the financial world. Money, after all, underpins it all.

Good luck.

LETTER TO MY OWN CHILDREN

While I may be a financial expert, I am also and always a mum, so I have written a note to my kids below. You might be able to relate to it.

Dear Cam and Maddy,

As a parent, I only want the best for you. I look at you both and I see a life you could live, success you could achieve, and equally the obstacles you are likely to face. It's my responsibility as your parent to help you to unlock your own potential, and to assist you in determining the path you want to walk and then to try to get you an inside lane. But it is up to you to walk it (or run it). Together we will try to increase the odds of finding the right path, but, even if it turns out it's not, being able to start again is a skill to be learned. The trick to life is to keep moving forward.

Life can be awesome, but it is often hard. People you think are your friends will not always be there when you need them. You will work for people who you will not always respect, and have the opportunity to exploit people or to be taken advantage of.

Hold your head, and your line.

Be honest.

The people you surround yourself with will inadvertently set you on a course to become more like them, so make sure you have good and smart people around you.

Treat others as you want to be treated.

Always be the hardest worker in the room. Too often people fail to unlock opportunity because it is dressed in overalls and looks like hard work. There is a smart way to progress fast, but there are no shortcuts. Doing the hard yards is part of the process of enjoying your rewards.

Do not dodge responsibility. Own your problems and work on how to be better. My wish is that you grow up to be righteous and resourceful. To be true and courageous.

Cam, don't get caught behind the bike shed smoking (or doing anything dodgy), ever.

Madison, you don't need a man to be successful. It will be harder for you to succeed, but that is why girls have been made just a little bit better than boys.

Be hard-working, humble and have just the right amount of hustle. It would also be great if you are financial rock stars, although no pressure.

Most importantly, learn to be happy and content. I will love you forever.

Love always,

Mum

SELECT BIBLIOGRAPHY

Books

Bateman, Katherine R. *The Young Investor: Projects and activities for making your money grow.* 2nd edn. Chicago: Chicago Review Press, Incorporated, 2001.

Bissonnette, Zac. *Debt-Free U: How I paid for an outstanding college education without loans, scholarships, or mooching off my parents.* New York: Portfolio Penguin, 2010.

Bowden, Sylvia. *How to Stop Your Kids from Going Broke.* Tauranga: Silbo Systems Ltd, 2009.

Challies, Tim. *Do More Better: A practical guide to productivity.* Minneapolis, MN: Cruciform Press, 2015.

Clinton, Timothy E., Bethany Palmer and Scott Palmer. *The Quick-Reference Guide to Counseling on Money, Finances & Relationships.* Grand Rapids, MI: Baker Books, 2012.

Damon, William. Greater Expectations: Overcoming the culture of indulgence in our homes and schools. New York: Simon & Schuster, Inc., 1996.

Duckworth, Angela. *Grit: The power of passion and perseverance.* New York: Scribner, 2016.

Duhigg, Charles. *Power of Habit: Why We Do What We Do in Life and Business.* New York: Random House Trade Paperbacks, 2012.

———. *Smarter Faster Better: The secrets of being productive in life and business.* New York: Random House, 2016.

Freud, Sigmund. *The Interpretation of Dreams.* Ed. Ritchie Robertson. Trans. Joyce Crick. Oxford: Oxford University Press, 1999.

Gladwell, Malcolm. *Blink: The power of thinking without thinking.* New York: Back Bay Books, 2007.

———. *David & Goliath: Underdogs, misfits, and the art of battling giants.* New York: Back Bay Books, 2015.

———. *Outliers: The story of success.* New York: Back Bay Books, 2008.

Godfrey, Joline. *Raising Financially Fit Kids*. 2nd edn. New York: Ten Speed Press, 2013.

Goldsmith, Marshall, Mark Reiter, Cullen Bunn and Shane Clester. *What Got You Here Won't Get You There*. Mundelein, IL: Writers of the Round Table Press/Round Table Comics, 2011.

Grant, Adam M. *Give and Take: A revolutionary approach to success*. New York: Viking, 2013.

Grant, Adam and Sheryl Sandberg. *Originals: How non-conformists change the world*. London, UK: WH Allen, 2016.

Hacker, Jacob S. *The Great Risk Shift: The new economic insecurity and the decline of the American dream*. Revised and expanded edn. Oxford: Oxford University Press, 2008.

Holiday, Ryan. *Ego Is the Enemy*. New York: Portfolio Penguin, 2016.

Hughes, Damian. *The Five STEPS to a Winning Mindset: What sport can teach us about great leadership*. London, UK: Pan Macmillan, 2016.

Jacobs, Jerry A. and Kathleen Gerson. *The Time Divide: Work, family, and gender inequality*. Cambridge, MA: Harvard University Press, 2004.

Kahneman, Daniel. *Thinking, Fast and Slow*. New York: Farrar, Straus and Giroux, 2011.

Kelley, David and Tom Kelley. *Creative Confidence: Unleashing the creative potential within us all*. New York: Crown Business, 2013.

Levitt, Steven D. and Stephen J. Dubner. *Freakonomics: A rogue economist explores the hidden side of everything*. New York: Harper Perennial, 2009.

Lieber, Ron. *The Opposite of Spoiled: Raising kids who are grounded, generous, and smart about money*. New York: HarperCollins, 2015.

Locke, John. *Some Thoughts Concerning Education*. Ed. John William Adamson. Mineola, NY: Dover Publications, Inc., 2007.

Martin, Steve J., Noah J. Goldstein and Robert B. Cialdini. *The Small BIG: Small changes that spark big influence*. New York: Hachette, 2014.

McQueen, Hannah. *Kill Your Mortgage and Sort Your Retirement: The go-to guide for getting ahead*. Auckland: Allen & Unwin, 2015.

————. *The Perfect Balance: How to get ahead financially and still have a life*. Auckland: Allen & Unwin, 2012.

Mischel, Walter. *The Marshmallow Test: Mastering self-control*. New York: Little, Brown and Company, 2014.

Murdock, Ruth. *Smart Kids: A parent's guide to raising financially healthy children*. Piara Waters, W.A.: Acorn Life Parth, 2015.

Oakley, Barbara A. *Cold-Blooded Kindness: Neuroquirks of a codependent killer, or just give me a shot at loving you, dear, and other reflections on helping that hurts*. Amherst, N.Y: Prometheus Books, 2011.

————. *Mindshift: Break through obstacles to learning and discover your hidden potential*. New York: Penguin Random House, 2017.

Orman, Suze. *The 9 Steps to Financial Freedom: Practical and spiritual steps so you can stop worrying*. 3rd edn. New York: Three Rivers Press, 2006.

————. *The Money Book for the Young, Fabulous & Broke*. New York: Riverhead Books, 2007.

————. *Women & Money: Owning the power to control your destiny*. New York: Spiegel & Grau, 2010.

Owen, David. *The First National Bank of Dad: A foolproof method for teaching your kids the value of money*. New York: Simon & Schuster, 2003.

Palmer, Scott and Bethany Palmer. *The 5 Money Conversations to Have with Your Kids at Every Age and Stage*. Nashville, TN: Thomas Nelson, 2014.

————. *The 5 Money Personalities: Speaking the same love and money language*. Nashville, TN: Thomas Nelson, 2013.

Piketty, Thomas. *The Economics of Inequality*. Cambridge, MA: Harvard University Press, 2015.

Pine, Karen Jane and Simonne Gnessen. *Sheconomics: Add power to your purse with the ultimate money makeover*. London: Headline Publishing Group, 2009.

Postman, Neil. *The Disappearance of Childhood*. New York: Random House, 1982.

Ramsey, Dave. *The Total Money Makeover: A proven plan for financial fitness*. Nashville, TN: Thomas Nelson, 2013.

Ramsey, Dave and Rachel Cruze. *Smart Money Smart Kids: Raising the next generation to win with money*. Brentwood, TN: Lampo Press, 2014.

Sember, Brette McWhorter. *The Everything Kids' Money Book: Earn It, Save It, and Watch It Grow!* Avon, MA: F+W Publications, Inc., 2008

Simonton, Dean Keith (ed.). *The Wiley Handbook of Genius*. Chichester, UK: John Wiley & Sons, Ltd, 2014.

Smith, Christian and Hilary A. Davidson. *The Paradox of Generosity: Giving we receive, grasping we lose*. New York: Oxford University Press, 2014.

Soon Lee, Michael and Grant Tabuchi. *Black Belt Negotiating: Become a master negotiator using powerful lessons from the martial arts*. New York: American Management Association, 2007.

Strong, Phil and Amanda van der Gulik. *Kids & Money: How to raise a financially savvy generation*. Hamilton, NZ: Wise Life LP, 2013.

Taleb, Nassim Nicholas. *Antifragile: Things that gain from disorder*. New York: Random House, 2012.

Whitburn, David. *Invest & Prosper with Property: How Kiwis can profit from property investment*. Auckland: Random House, 2011.

Articles and reports

'2011 Teens & Money Survey Findings: Insights into money attitudes, behaviors and expectations of 16- to 18-year-olds.' Charles Schwab & Co., Inc., 2011.

'Children with more self-control turn into healthier and wealthier adults.' University of Otago. <www.otago.ac.nz/news/news/otago016129.html>

Claus, Iris, Paul Kilford, Geoff Leggett and Xin Wang. 'Costs of raising children.' Report for the Official Statistics Forum 2010. <www.stats. govt.nz/~/media/Statistics/about-us/statisphere/Files/os-forum-2010/2-1450-iris-claus.pdf>

Baer, Drake and Rachel Gillet. 'Science says parents of successful kids have these 11 things in common.' *Business Insider Australia*, 30 November 2015. <www.businessinsider.com.au/how-parents-set-their-

kids-up-for-success-2015-11?r=US&IR=T#/#1-they-make-their-kids-do-chores-2>

Barnea, Amir, Henrik Cronqvist and Stephan Siegel. 'Nature or nurture: what determines investor behavior?' *Journal of Financial Economics.* December 2010, vol. 98, no. 3, pp. 583–604.

Begley, Sharon. 'The new science behind your spending addiction.' *Newsweek*, 30 October 2011. <europe.newsweek.com/new-science-behind-your-spending-addiction-68063>

Belk, Russell W., Clifford Rice and Randall Harvey. 'Adolescents' reported saving, giving, and spending as a function of sources of income.' *Advances in Consumer Research*, 1985, vol. 12, pp. 42–6. Eds Elizabeth C. Hirschman and Moris B. Holbrook. Provo: Association for Consumer Research.

Boulding, William and Markus Christen. 'Sustainable pioneering advantage? profit implications of market entry order.' *Marketing Science*, August 2003, vol. 22, no. 3, pp. 371–92.

Briody, Blaire. 'When parents pay for college, could kids' grades suffer?' *The Week*, 23 January 2013. <theweek.com/articles/468505/when-parents-pay-college-could-kids-grades-suffer>

Cantillon, Richard. 'Essai sur la nature du commerce en Général.' Translated as 'An essay on Economic theory' by Chantal Saucier. Alabama: Ludwig von Mises Institute, 2010.

Carver, Charles S. and Teri L. White. 'Behavioral inhibition, behavioral activation, and affective responses to impending reward and punishment: the BIS/BAS scales.' *Journal of Personality and Social Psychology*, 1994, vol. 67, pp. 319–33.

Dell'Antonia, KJ. 'Age-appropriate chores for children (and why they're not doing them).' Motherlode blog, *The New York Times*, 27 January 2014. <parenting.blogs.nytimes.com/2014/01/27/age-appropriate-chores-for-children-and-why-theyre-not-doing-them>

Dobrev, Stanislav D. and Aleksios Gotsopoulos. 'Legitimacy vacuum, structural imprinting, and the first mover disadvantage.' *Academy of Management Journal*, October 2010, vol. 53, no. 5, pp. 1153–74.

Dooley, Roger. 'Priming the customer.' Neuromarketing, 6 April 2006. <www.neurosciencemarketing.com/blog/articles/priming-the-customer.htm>

Feist, Gregory J. and Frank X. Barron. 'Predicting creativity from early to late adulthood: Intellect, potential, and personality.' *Journal of Research in Personality*, 2003, vol. 37, no. 2, pp. 62–88.

Gandel, Stephen. 'Everything you know about kids and money is wrong.' *Money*, August 2006, vol. 35, no. 8, pp. 112.

Golder, Peter N. and Gerard J. Tellis. 'Pioneer advantage: Marketing logic or marketing legend?' *Journal of Marketing Research*, 1993, vol. 30, no. 2, pp. 158–70.

Hamilton, Laura T. 'More is more or more is less? Parental financial investments during college.' *American Sociological Review*, February 2013, vol. 78, no, pp. 70–95.

'How Banks Create Money.' *Positive Money*. <positivemoney.org/how-money-works/how-banks-create-money/>

Lewin, Elizabeth S. and Bernard Ryan Jr. 'How to Raise Money-Smart Kids.' *Your Money*, October/November 1995, vol. 16, no. 6. Republished on Kids' Money. <www.kidsmoney.org/allart5.htm>

McLeay, Michael, Amar Radia, and Ryland Thomas. 'Money creation in the modern economy.' Bank of England Quarterly Bulletin 2014, vol. 54, no. 1, pp. 4–12.

Moffitt, Terrie E., Louise Arseneault, Daniel Belsky, Nigel Dickson, Robert J. Hancox, HonaLee Harrington, Renate Houts, et al. 'A gradient of childhood self-control predicts health, wealth, and public safety.' *Proceedings of the National Academy of Sciences*, 15 February 2011, vol. 108, no. 7, pp. 2693–98.

Murdock, Jason. 'Sweden's central bank turns to national digital currency as society ditches cash.' *International Business Times*, 17 November 2016. <www.ibtimes.co.uk/swedens-central-bank-turns-national-digital-currency-society-ditches-cash-1592083>

Natale, Carl. 'How to successfully negotiate lower prices in any situation', *Money Crashers*. <www.moneycrashers.com/successfully-negotiate-lower-prices/>

'Natural stock selection: A new excuse for lousy investors.' *The Economist*, 10 March 2012. <www.economist.com/node/21549970>

Nemeth, Charlan J., Bernard Personnaz, Marie Personnaz and Jack A. Goncalo. 'The liberating role of conflict in group creativity: A study in two countries.' *ResearchGate*, 1 July 2004, vol. 34, no. 4, pp. 365–74.

'Number of businesses owned by women skyrockets.' MYOB, 12 October 2016. <www.myob.com/nz/about/news/2016/number-of-businesses-owned-by-women-skyrockets>

'On misemployment.' *The Book of Life*. <www.thebookoflife.org/unemployment-down-at-last-misemployment-bad-as-ever/>

Palmer, Kate. 'Your genes decide if you're good at saving money, academics say.' *The Telegraph*, 26 February 2015. <www.telegraph.co.uk/finance/personalfinance/savings/11436282/Your-genes-decide-if-youre-good-at-saving-money-academics-say.html>

Pham, Tam. 'Are you planning to quit your day job to start your business? Think again . . .' *The Hustle*, 22 February 2016. <thehustle.co/are-you-planning-to-quit-your-day-job-to-start-your-business-think-again>

Pine, Karen J. 'Report on a survey into female economic behaviour and the emotion regulatory role of spending.' Sheconomics Survey Report 2009. Hatfield, UK: University of Hertfordshire, 2009.

Quinn, Patrick D. and Kim Fromme. 'Alcohol use and related problems among college students and their noncollege peers: The competing roles of personality and peer influence.' *Journal of Studies on Alcohol and Drugs*, July 2011, vol. 72, no. 4, pp. 622–32.

Rick, Scott I., Cynthia E. Cryder and George Loewenstein. 'Tightwads and spendthrifts.' *Journal of Consumer Research*, April 2008, vol. 34, no. 6, pp. 767–82.

Roberts, M. B. 'Could procrastinating reveal your most creative thoughts?' *Parade*, 2 February 2016. <parade.com/453486/m-b-roberts/why-you-should-procrastinate/>

Savitsky, Kenneth, Victoria Husted Medvec and Thomas Gilovich. 'Remembering and regretting: The Zeigarnik effect and the cognitive availability of regrettable actions and inactions.' *Personality and Social Psychology Bulletin*, March 1997, vol. 23, no.3, pp. 248–57.

Schwab-Pomerantz, Carrie. 'Is your teen financially fit?' Charles Schwab, 24 August 2016. <www.schwab.com/public/schwab/nn/articles/Is-Your-Teen-Financially-Fit>

Seltzer, Rick. 'Parents spend more time talking about money with boys than girls.' *Baltimore Business Journal*, 18 August 2014. <www.bizjournals.com/baltimore/news/2014/08/18/parents-spend-more-time-talking-about-money-with.html>

Shin, Laura. 'The 5 most important money lessons to teach your kids.' *Forbes*, 15 October 2013. <www.forbes.com/sites/laurashin/2013/10/15/the-5-most-important-money-lessons-to-teach-your-kids/>

Simonton, Dean Keith. 'Creative productivity: A predictive and explanatory model of career trajectories and landmarks.' *Psychological Review*, 1997, vol. 104, no. 1, pp. 66–89.

Smolensky, Eugene and Jennifer Appleton Gootman (eds). *Working Families and Growing Kids: caring for children and adolescents*. Washington, D.C.: National Academies Press, 2003.

Somers, Jan. *More Wealth from Residential Property*. Cleveland, Australia: Somerset Financial Services, 2001.

Surowiecki, James. 'Epic fails of the startup world.' *The New Yorker*, 19 May 2014. <www.newyorker.com/magazine/2014/05/19/epic-fails-of-the-startup-world>

'Teens and Personal Finance Survey: Executive summary.' Junior Achievement USA®/Allstate Foundation, 2012. <www.ja.org>

'The Marshmallow Study Revisited.' University of Rochester, 11 October 2012. <www.rochester.edu/news/show.php?id=4622>

'Upromise releases new study on the effects of working while in college.' *PR Newswire*, 27 August 2001. <www.prnewswire.com/news-releases/upromise-releases-new-study-on-the-effects-of-working-while-in-college-71836792.html>

Urist, Jacob. 'What the marshmallow test really teaches about self-control.' *The Atlantic*, 24 September 2014. <www.theatlantic.com/health/archive/2014/09/what-the-marshmallow-test-really-teaches-about-self-control/380673/>

Xu, Hongwei and Martin Ruef. 'The myth of the risk-tolerant entrepreneur.' *Strategic Organization*, 1 November 2004, vol. 2, no. 4, pp. 331–55.

Zhang, Zhen, and Richard D. Arvey. 'Rule breaking in adolescence and entrepreneurial status: An empirical investigation.' *Journal of Business Venturing*, September 2009, vol. 24, no. 5, pp. 436–47.

Talks

Lythcott-Haims, Julie. 'How to raise successful kids—without over-parenting.' Talk given at TED Talks Live in New York, November 2015. <www.ted.com/talks/julie_lythcott_haims_how_to_raise_successful_kids_without_over_parenting>

Moffitt, Terrie. 'Young children's self-control and the health and wealth of their nation.' Keynote address delivered 13 March 2015 at the inaugural International Convention of Psychological Science. <www.youtube.com/watch?v=KT9otL6pxKQ>

Poulton, Richie. 'Looking through the lens of 1000 Lives.' Talk given at TEDxDunedin on 5 July 2012. <www.ted.com/tedx/events/6169>

Websites

Empathy design studio. <www.empathydesign.com>

enableMe. <enableme.co.nz>

New Zealand Association of Economists blog. <www.nzae.org.nz>

Sorted. <www.sorted.org.nz>

SPECIAL THANKS

This book has been hard work, and I am not sure I would have achieved it without the support of many people. My executive assistant, Natalie, and the team at Allen & Unwin have been wonderful, persistent and tolerant (in equal measures!) in helping me to create an end product that I am proud of. Sarah Ell has been amazing, and very patient. Bernice Tuffery's help with research and interviewing different people has been invaluable. Special thanks to John Cowan of The Parenting Place and to Diane Levy, Mt Albert Grammar, Kubi Witten-Hannah, Catherine McIntyre, Sam Howard, Greg Fenton, Jacqui Pearse, Glenys Sparling-Fenton, and all the students who I interviewed or who completed surveys. A special mention and thanks to my old college, Havelock North High School, and to the students who helped me understand the mind of a teenager. Thank you.

At enableMe, I work with an incredible bunch of people who are committed to helping others understand and unlock their financial capability. They share my vision of improving the financial future of Kiwis by providing practical advice, financial smarts and support, using a proven (and patented) methodology to create positive change in our clients' lives. I am proud of the business we have built, and I am even prouder of the around 50 people who make up our team. We may be small, but we are mighty!

To the working mums everywhere—we are in this together.

Most importantly, to my husband, Billy, to my parents and to my wonderful (but often naughty) children, Madison and Cameron. I do it for you.

SPECIAL OFFER

I would like to offer a discounted first meeting with an enableMe Financial Personal Trainer to readers of this book who would like help getting ahead faster—especially those who need to make sure they have their own financial strategy in place before they can preach the benefits of doing the same to their kids!

In this meeting, we will work together to ascertain where you are at financially, where you want to be, and whether it is possible for you to reach your goals faster. It will then be up to you whether or not you wish to continue working with us from that point. Either way, the outcome of your first meeting will be that you will know your capabilities; your next step will be to unlock them. Visit www.enableme.co.nz to request a consultation, and make sure to mention that you have read this book.

Note that I will also be launching a financial coaching programme for teenagers towards the end of 2017. This programme will offer teens real-life skills to prepare them for financial success in adulthood. Stay tuned!